MIKE LIPKIN

on Fire!

The Art Of Personal Consistency

How To Always Play At Your Personal Best, When It Counts.

ENVIRONICS/LIPKIN
RESEARCHED MOTIVATION & PERSUASION

On
The Art Of
Personal
Consistency
Fire!

On Fire! The Art of Personal Consistency
Copyright 2004 by Mike Lipkin
First edition in 2004 by Environics/Lipkin

33 Bloor Street East, Suite 900
Toronto, Ontario
Canada M4W 3H1

Design & layout by Maria Emery.
Printed in Canada

www.mikelipkin.com

contents

LIVE IN THE
SWEET
SPOT.

Hello!

I know you don't have much time so I'll cut straight to the chase. This is a book about your biggest challenge: how to always perform at Your Personal Best when it counts.

No one can be on all the time. It's not possible and it may not even be desirable. It's about being on when you really need to be on – when the stakes are high and other people are depending on your play.

It's about the certainty and serenity that comes from knowing you'll bring out your best game in the most important games. It's about the post-event high that follows a best-you-can-deliver performance. It's about living in that place called the edge-of-your-capacity: the point you know is as far as you can go in that moment.

It's about addiction to **stretch:** the constant tautness of becoming more by being more right now. It's about the insights, the strategies and the stories of People-On-Fire: The people who consistently do the things that inspire us to want to do the same. Most importantly, this book is about Your-Way: your unique plan for becoming More-You.

Here's my promise:
On Fire! will give you what leaders all over the world have told me is their #1 ask of their people: to be on all-times-when-it-counts, not some-times-when-it-counts.

It *is* possible. In fact, it's the Platinum Standard of the Best-in-Class Champions.

Think about it: how would you feel about me if I was introduced as follows, "Ladies and

Gentlemen, please welcome Mr. Mike Lipkin, one of the world's great motivators...when he's on"? Exactly. You would laugh.

I make a living being Always On. I stand in front of people and I talk. No notes. No PowerPoint. No props. Just me and the audience for an hour, a morning or a day.

My audience doesn't much care about my problems, my past or my paranoias. They don't care about the talk before theirs or the one after. All they care about is getting the good stuff from me in the moment.

So I have no choice. My entire career depends on every talk. Many people will only see me once and that's their lifelong impression of who I am. One off-day can be the beginning of oblivion.

What's the difference between you and me? Nothing. If you're not On Fire, you will be fired. Maybe not today or even tomorrow. But it will happen. You will be fired one client at a time as they warm to someone else's Personal Heat.

How hot are you? How much passion do you radiate? Are you sustaining your PBMs (Personal Best Moments)? Or are they few and far between? Are you described as consistently outstanding? Or are you merely intermittent?

How strong is your internal need to consistently perform at your Personal Best? Powerful and Pulsating? Or Maybe and Maybe Not?

If, like me, you belong to the Cult of Always-On, your desire to be the Best-You-That-You-Can-Be is your driving force. It's what thrills, excites and delights you. And that's precisely what this book will do.

**LIVE IN THE
SWEET
SPOT.**

The Spirit and Substance of *On Fire!*

"How can I stay as turned-on as I feel right now?" is the most common question I'm asked during or after a motivational program.

It's ironic, but even as delegates experience the High-of-What's-Possible, they're already anticipating the Low-of-When-I-Get-Back-to-the-Office.

It's sad. The vast majority of delegates (over 80 per cent) believe that a highly motivated state is not the norm for them. Rather, their norm is a state of anxiety, tension, crisis or stress. Even when they like what they're doing, they often feel overwhelmed by their life and work.

Well, here's the Spirit of this book: **On Fire means that being highly motivated, excited and inspired can and should be your natural state.** Anything else should be seen as a deviation from the norm.

Instinctively, how did you respond to the above statement? Did you nod your head in agreement? Or did you shake your head in incredulity?

If you're in agreement, the rest of this book is merely about execution.

If you're incredulous, I hope to overcome your skepticism with facts, stories, people, insights and strategies that are so powerful you'll believe being On Fire is possible. Maybe, just maybe, you'll even believe it's probable.

Whatever your current mental posture, and wherever you end up at the conclusion of this book, here's a fact that cannot be disputed: the most consistent person always triumphs in the end. As the advertisement for Accenture states: "High performers know it's not whether you win or lose. It's whether you keep on winning."

In fact, consistently outstanding performance is the new benchmark of champions. As David Aisenstat, CEO of Keg Restaurants, states, "To get to 90 per cent customer satisfaction is just the entry level. It's getting the last details to get to 98, 99, 100 per cent satisfaction levels. Today, you have to be so good, so consistent to be successful."

Like any good entrepreneur, I respond strongly and quickly to glaring client needs. So when client after client asked me if I could help them improve their people's level of Personal Consistency, I researched available resources.

I scanned the Net, scoured Amazon and took counsel from my personal board of directors. I couldn't find anything that single-mindedly focused on being Always On.

Then, in the cathartic heat of a luxurious bath, I had a BFO – a Blinding Flash of the Obvious. Nothing had been created because I knew that I was meant to create it. Personal Consistency is what I live and breathe.

On Fire has been gestating for a year. Together with my assistant, Erica Cerny, we've researched the gestalt of Personal Consistency. We've studied the lives and actions of people who epitomize it. I've spoken to people throughout the United States, Canada, Europe and Africa who exude it. And, with the help of my favourite digital scout, Google, I've searched the universe for examples that exemplify it.

From June 2003 to March 2004, we also methodically scanned the *Wall Street Journal*, the *New York Times, USA Today*, the *Globe and Mail*, the *National Post*, the *Toronto Star* and the *Financial Times* for real-time accounts of both the trends shaping the environment and the people who were achieving the highest levels of Personal Consistency.

Overlaying all this data is the proprietary Environics 3SC Social Values Monitor. By tracking people aged 15 and older, the 3SC Monitor identifies consumer motivations and relationships to brands, products and services. Organizations worldwide use it to understand consumers, define social policy and establish human resource strategies.

The 3SC Monitor analyzes social trends using more than 200 questions to probe social values and beliefs. The resulting trends are placed on a sociocultural map and their specific movements tracked against a wide variety of geographic, demographic and attitudinal benchmarks. The 3SC Monitor has measured trends in Canada since 1983 and in the United States since 1992. It is a unique international tool that allows clients to link national research to parallel research from 20 countries around the world.

The 3SC Monitor allows me to place The Art of Personal Consistency in the context of environmental shifts, especially in the U.S. and Canada. As you'll see, the demand for People-On-Fire has never been greater. And the supply is building to meet demand.

Purpose, Design and Function

The purpose of this book is simple: to turn you into a Person-On-Fire. Anyone else will not thrive in an environment that is becoming more demanding, more chaotic, more surprise-driven by the hour.

You never know when and you never know where your next Big Opportunity will appear. What you do know with total certainty is that if you're not ready for it, it will go to someone else. Opportunities are never lost; they are just taken by others.

Here's what I know: it's only when you're motivated, excited and inspired that you can be All You. **Without the energy generated by a turned-on state, big chunks of You are left unused.** A Person-On-Fire will always trump someone who is lukewarm.

So this book has been designed with one constant mandate in mind: to make it easy for you to ignite. I want you to get it immediately. I want all your energy directed towards applying what you read, not trying to understand what you've read.

I also promise you this: you'll stay with me until the very last word because I'll grip your imagination with insights that are so compelling, you'll find it impossible to let go. These are not just outputs of my imagination. Because of my craft as a professional speaker, I spend my time with the best and brightest people in the world. That's all I do – talk to people, record my thoughts and offer them to others. I'm on a permanent diet of inspiration and empowerment.

Eventually we all become the company we keep. So the more time I spend with inspired people, the more inspired I become. In turn, I want to pay it forward. As Nelson Mandela said, "As you let your own light shine, you unconsciously give others permission to do the same."

Like any great joint venture, this book is a partnership between you and me. So at the beginning of each section, I'll give you a Self-Exploration to complete. This is a series of questions that I want you to answer instinctively. Simply write down the first response that presents itself to you. Each Self-Exploration will take you no more than a few seconds, but it will give you an immediate sense of your beliefs and attitudes towards the issues that follow.

Don't overthink the Self-Explorations. Listen to your intuition. Record your response and move on. Come back to them after you've finished the book and applied its lessons. You'll be amazed at how far the needle will move.

Today's wisdom is tomorrow's roadkill.

You'll see throughout the book that I've used the Socratic Method of motivation and learning. The Socratic Method, originally employed by the Greek philosopher Socrates, is the use of questions to help respondents develop ideas and conclusions in their own minds. By leading my clients, colleagues, friends or relatives through a series of focused questions, I help them facilitate their "AHAs." They take ownership of their breakthroughs.

I know I don't have the answers. In fact, I don't even look for answers any more. **In a high velocity age, answers have a shorter life span than a squirrel trying to cross an eight-lane highway.** Today's wisdom is tomorrow's roadkill.

Instead, I'm trying to ask the right questions. All progress begins with someone asking the right question. Questions become both your focus and your filter. In fact, right now you're asking yourself a series of questions: what does this mean to me? How can I use this? Why am I even reading this? How can I share this? How relevant is this point to my life?

Are you a Great Question Asker? Do you lead your stakeholders through a process of self-discovery as you highlight the range of possibilities available to them that they would not have identified on their own? Observe the effective influencers around you. Listen to the way they get their subjects to reach their desired conclusion. They ask questions 80 per cent of the time.

So stay with me. Together, we'll ask the questions that help create Your-Way: your unique plan for becoming More-You. Because if you don't have a plan for your life, who does? In fact, if you don't have a plan for your life, you'll live a plan that someone else may have for you. And it may not be designed with your best interests in mind.

The Bedrock of Personal Consistency: Fresh-minded Repetition

At its essence, Personal Consistency is the relentless adherence to a set of defining behaviours. It's an unswerving commitment to a life-course. It's also a simple function of what you do most often every day. Eventually we become our actions. We become more of what we do.

1. Focus. 2. Expect More. 3. Be You. 4. Play Full Out. 5. Make World-Class Friends. 6. Learn and Let Go.

These are the six steps to catching fire and staying combusted. The more times you take them, the better you become. Execution is the pathway to excellence.

The less you have to think about in life's make-or-break moments, the more thought you can apply to being Your Personal Best when it counts. That's when your conditioning kicks in. And that's why People-On-Fire thrive when others tank. They've done the hard work ahead of time. They're performance-ready. They bring more capacity to their challenges. Their minds are not clogged with doubts and uncertainties.

Repetition is the mother of learning. Repetition is the mother of learning. Repetition...You've got the message. Not mindless repetition. That's the pathway to staleness. It's the antithesis of learning.

I'm talking about Fresh-Minded Repetition. This is where you consciously take the actions that produce results over and over again. And each time you act, you think about what you're doing with a Fresh Mind — an appreciation of the impact of your activity combined with a curiosity of how you could make it even more forceful.

I apply the concept of Fresh-Minded Repetition even when it comes to walking. I became aware of my mortality for the first time in December 2001. After many years of intense physical activity, I was fit but damaged. I had herniated a disc between my L4 and L5 vertebrae. These are the two lowest vertebrae. As a result, I needed a spinal fusion. Briefly, this is a process whereby a titanium pin is inserted into the vertebrae and, over time, the bone fuses.

As the surgeon congratulated me on the success of the operation and described the healing process, I remember thinking about how I was now part bone and part metal. I remembered thinking about how without medical science, I would be condemned to a life of pain and immobility. And I remembered wondering how many more repairs my physical machine would need before my three score years and ten expired.

Then something extraordinary happened. I walked. Seriously. The surgeon instructed me to walk within 48 hours of the operation in order to accelerate my recovery. As I took a few faltering steps around the hospital ward, everyone applauded – the doctor, the nurse, my wife, my children. How weird, I thought. The last time this happened to me, I was 11 months old. I felt both pristine and prematurely feeble at the same time. Hmmm, time to begin again from scratch, I thought. And the next month, I immigrated to Canada. Three years later, I still revel in being able to walk long distances without the pain of a pinched nerve crippling me.

Throughout my ten year career as an international motivator, there has been a central theme to the "AHA moments," epiphanies and breakthroughs experienced by people who have gone on to lead awe-inspiring lives: they all had a defining turnaround moment.

For some, it was a chance meeting with an extraordinary soul. For others, it was a lightning flash of inspiration in the middle of the night. For others it was a wake-up call through illness or an almost fatal accident. For still others it was a connection with their higher power. My point is that something or someone triggered a Whole New Level of awareness, action and accountability that set these People-On-Fire. In the next few pages, I hope that happens to you.

The great British poet, TS Eliot said it best: **"Throughout our lives, we should not cease from exploring. And the end of our exploring shall be to arrive back where we started and to know that place for the first time."**

See the world with fresh eyes every day and you'll see further. Those who dream by day, said Edgar Allan Poe, see far more than those who only dream by night.

There is an old Zen saying, "Before enlightenment, chop wood, draw water. After enlightenment, chop wood, draw water." Post-enlightenment, the chopping of wood and the drawing of water is a very different experience. In fact, it's the difference between being extinguished and being On Fire. So be enlightened. Discern the potential of every act. Go further by seeing further.

Lipkin's Definition of Happiness: closing the gap between what is and what should be.

I'm in the business of making people happy. So think about it: when are you truly happy? Isn't it when things are exactly the way you want them to be? Isn't it when there's no gap between the way things are and the way you believe they ought to be? Those things can be external or internal. And while you may have minimal control over your external factors, you have total control over what's going inside of you.

Mastering the Art of Personal Consistency means eliminating or narrowing the internal gap between what is and what should be. And that's what this book is really all about: the satisfaction that comes with knowing you're being the-most-you-can-be at any given moment. Remove the gap between you and Your Personal Best and you remove the gap between you and Your Personal Happiness.

The Social Environment in 2004 and Beyond

2003 was a record year for crises on an unprecedented scale: viruses, floods, wars, fires, storms, mad cows, terrorist threats and blackouts rolled over the continent in an apocalyptic wave.

On a micro-level, people's stress was exacerbated by the insatiable corporate drive for More-With-Less. Despite outstanding top-line results, companies focused relentlessly on cost containment while exhorting their people to raise their levels of productivity.

And yet, in 2003, a peculiar thing happened: people's level of motivation and optimism rose. After six years of growing disillusionment and rising feelings of exclusion, Environics research reveals a strong directional change.

Americans and Canadians are accepting the certainty of uncertainty. Despite persistent anxiety, a more resilient social fabric is emerging. People are relearning how to live with insecurity carefully and pragmatically.

People's view of the economic situation is improving. Optimism about both their own and their country's financial outlook is increasing.

This optimism is reflected in their greater energy and more proactive attitudes. More and more of us are taking charge of our lives in order to find a better personal balance.

We're opening up. We're reinventing ourselves. Personal creativity has become important again. We're daring to believe in our dreams once more.

Hearth and home is becoming even more important as people try to create their "Personal Bubble" – that safe, private place where they can recharge their emotional batteries and draw on their inner resources.

In both Canada and the United States, people remain cautious. They're taking only calculated risks in their pursuit of success so as not to unduly threaten the personal balance and security they're trying so hard to achieve.

Personal Growth is making a comeback. Goals are reasserting themselves. People are daring to set personal targets and go after them pragmatically and selectively. In response to the demand for greater personal productivity, enthusiasm for technology is returning. Usage of the Internet, time management devices and mobile technology are all increasing.

People's renewed sense of vitality is also reflecting itself notably in stronger feelings of belonging – to social networks, the community at large and even to their country.

On both sides of the border, people's attachment to their country's values has increased in response to alien and hostile cultures exposed daily in the media.

A greater openness to others is also showing itself in more attention being paid to ecological and social issues. In fact, a more ethical approach in general to both business and consumption is being embraced.

Simplicity and authenticity is in. People want products that meet their fundamental needs. Ostentation is out. Products or services that help people achieve their personal ambitions and enhance their personal power are also in increasing demand.

If we bring it all together, according to the Environics research, there are three themes that will characterize the next 24 to 36 months:

First Theme:
The Return of Belief-in-Self: Renewed Vitality, Self-Assertiveness and Personal Investment

People are demonstrating a growing ability to deal with uncertainty. Aware that they should not have unrealistic expectations about the world in which they evolve, people are discovering new resources within themselves in their quest for personal development.

We are becoming less fatalistic. We're more aware of our options in advancing despite an environment that we still perceive as threatening.

Our private space is a place to which we go not just for rest and relaxation, but also for recharging and renewal. It's where we focus on our new priorities of well-being and personal harmony.

We're leading a healthier lifestyle, both in terms of diet and exercise. This is driven by the desire to look and feel good, but it's also a function of our increased desire to take control of our personal destinies. Good health is now seen as an essential requirement for future success.

According to *USA Today* (12/31/03), the top three categories of New Year's resolutions are Health and Fitness (22%), Career (18%), Personal Growth (15%). What's more, consumers are putting their money where their resolutions are. Retail trends show a strong undercurrent of consumer interest that's moving away from stuff for stuff's sake and towards stuff that makes recipients feel healthy, think clearly or even appear ageless. And what's driving this trend is aging Baby Boomers demanding a better, often healthier lifestyle for themselves and their kids. (*USA Today* 11/30/03)

The trend is even showing up in Costco. One of the hot sellers at the warehouse chain is a $39 gift basket loaded with creams, lotions and moisturizers. "We sell every one of the baskets that we put out there," says CEO Jim Sinegal. The story is the same for the antithesis of Costco: Neiman Marcus. Among the upscale chain's bestsellers are a $132 Juicy Couture gym bag, a $135 tube of Natura Inhibit wrinkle fighting cream, and a $195 yoga kit with a Neiman Marcus engraved mat, bag and strap.

Sales of performance and fitness equipment are also up strongly. "There's a big shift going on among kids who are less interested in being computer geeks and more interested in playing sports," says Steve Modell, CEO of Modell's Sporting Goods. Ditto for their parents. Fitness equipment sales topped $4.3 billion in 2003, up more than 10 per cent from the year before. As Boomers age, "Many distrust the potential of medicine to keep them healthy but are very concerned about staying alive and well," says Thomas Doyle, Vice President of Research at the National Sporting Goods Association.

Along with a more optimistic mindset is a rise in Personal Creativity. This is defined as a desire to use one's imagination and creative talents in daily life, both at work and at play. More and more people want to give free rein to their dreams and ambitions. They're becoming more flexible in adapting to the New Normal.

The *New York Times* (08/31/03) reported on a new psychographic: Rejuveniles. These are grown-ups who cultivate juvenile tastes in products and entertainment. They're "kidults" – adults who take care of the kid inside them.

So, for example, the average age of video game players is now 29, up from 18 in 1990. Puma, Converse and Keds sneakers have leapt from the schoolyard set to the fashion conscious crowd. Tony Hawk, the skateboard icon and hero to adolescent boys everywhere, is 35 years old. Harry Potter's cross-generational popularity prompted its publisher, Bloomsbury, to release an issue with so-called "grown-up covers."

Increasingly, forty and fifty something's wear the same clothes as their teenage children, listen to the same music and thrill to the same technology – witness the iPod's ageless appeal. Hip, lovable, sexy, colourful, fun, and active are in. As the advertisement for Durex Condoms urges: Grow Old Disgracefully.

Bryan Page, a professor of Anthropology at the University of Miami, states it well when he says, "Play has historically been about recreation or preparing children to move into adult roles. That whole dynamic has been reversed – **play has become the primary purpose and value in many adult lives. It now borders on the sacred.** From a historical standpoint, that's entirely backward."

This rise in Personal Creativity is not just a want-to-do in the home space, it's a have-to-do in the workplace. As Robert Reich, former U.S. secretary of labour and professor of social and economic policy at Brandeis, states in the *Wall Street Journal* (12/26/03), "Any job that's even slightly routine is disappearing from the U.S. But this doesn't mean we are left with fewer jobs. It means only that we have fewer routine jobs. The problem isn't the number of jobs in America; it's the quality of jobs. Look closely at the economy today and you find two growing categories of work – but only the first is commanding better pay and benefits. This category involves identifying and solving new problems. Here workers do R&D, design and engineering. Or they're responsible for high level sales, marketing and advertising. They're composers, writers and producers. They're lawyers, bankers, financiers, journalists, doctors and management consultants."

Reich continues, "I call this 'symbolic analytic' work because most of it has to do with analyzing, manipulating and communicating through numbers, shapes, words, ideas. There's no necessary limit to the number of symbolic analytic jobs because there's no finite limit to the ingenuity of the mind or to human needs."

"The second growing category of work in America involves personal-services," states Reich, "Computers and robots can't do these jobs because they require care or attentiveness. Workers in other nations can't do them because they must be done in person. Some personal-services workers need education beyond high school – nurses, physical therapists, medical technicians for example. But most don't, such as restaurant workers, cabbies, retail workers, security guards, and hospital attendants. In contrast to that of symbolic analysts, the pay of most personal-service workers in the U.S. is stagnant or declining. That's because the supply of personal-service workers is growing quickly as more and more people who'd otherwise have factory or routine service jobs join their ranks."

If you want to truly live well, therefore, you have to differentiate yourself by enhancing your value to others through

consistent innovation, imagination and bold actions. Routine equals danger — danger of oblivion, obsolescence and obscurity. Personal breakthroughs need to become everyday events. The new client-service benchmark is "Give me the edge that will make me successful in my business. Tell me something I don't know so I can do something I couldn't do before. And keep telling me so I can keep doing it."

Flexibility of Gender Identity

We're witnessing the rise of "Metro-Sexuality." There is a greater acceptance of both the male and female sides of our sexuality. We're becoming more aware of our feelings and we refuse to be trapped in traditional roles where male and female traits are theoretically incompatible.

The *Queer Eye for the Straight Guy* is making guys who are even marginally on-trend more fashionable and stylish. Even the most masculine of us are becoming comfortable with gel, moisturizer, clothing consultants and other accouterments of the New Acceptable Narcissism. It's now acceptable for men (including me, I might add), to pamper themselves at a spa and apply nightly moisturizers without impugning their manhood. In fact, being metrosexual in a gender-equality era has become decidedly sexy.

As William Safire writes in the *New York Times Magazine* (12/7/03), "The celebrity most associated with the word (Metrosexual) is David Beckham, captain of England's soccer team. The beloved "Becks" wears designer clothes off the field, has been seen in sarongs and nail polish and boasts a different hairstyle every week. He is proudly and indisputably a dandy, comfortable with what is called his 'feminine side'."

Women, on the other hand, are increasingly demonstrating the traditional male traits of leadership, career ambition and professional networking. In fact, we're witnessing a new generation of "female jocks" as their leadership style and conflict resolution becomes more and more suited to an uncertain, ambiguous future.

From the workspace to the home place, women are usurping men. Even big box hardware stores, the long-established domain of "home improvement" handymen, now woo women as their key target market. Pat Wilkinson, Director of Marketing at Home Depot Canada, says that women account for 50 per cent of all spending.

Narcissism is Nice

If the mantra of the eighties was "Greed is Good," the creed of this decade is "Narcissism is Nice," even for guys. You know why? Because when we're around people whom look and feel good, vicariously we feel the same way. And even our inevitable occasional feelings of envy have a purpose: they motivate us to want to look and feel similar.

Thirty years ago, reports the *Toronto Star* (01/10/04), it took $6 million to make the Bionic Man. Today, a mere $5000 and a razor cut get you a New Man (or New Woman). Fantasy has always been television's bread and butter but today's viewers are turning it into reality, embracing the shows about transformation – *Extreme Makeover*, *The Swan*, and *Nip/Tuck* for example. Enhanced technology, surgical skills and increasing social acceptance of personal "body sculpting," mean that acquiring the face, the body and even the personality you want is only a few dollars and little pain away.

According to the *Toronto Star* (01/10/04), in the U.S., between 1997 and 2002, breast implant surgery increased 147 per cent, liposuction rose 111 per cent, and eyelid surgery increased 44 per cent. Add in non-surgical procedures such as Botox treatments, and cosmetic procedures in the U.S. were up 226 per cent over the five-year period.

Beyond the surgical or pharmaceutical panacea, ageing Baby Boomers and "elders" are working hard at building their physical beauty. Here are some extraordinary stats from the U.S. health club industry: since 1987, 18-34 year-olds, the traditional mainstays of the industry have grown by only 27 per cent, to 11.5 million members. Baby Boomers aged 35-54 now account for 12.4 million members. In absolute terms, their numbers have jumped by 135 per cent since 1987. As a percentage of the population, 15.2 out of every 100 people in this age group are health club members, up from only 9.5 in 1987.

Over the past 15 years, the defining characteristic of industry change has been the growth in the population of older health club members. In 2001, there were 5.6 million members over the age of 55, representing an absolute increase of 266 per cent over 1987.

For better or for worse, we are all influenced more than we should be by physical beauty. But it goes beyond physical beauty alone. We are attracted to physical vitality. There's an aura that fit people have about them. They have an alertness and readiness for action that makes them natural leaders, especially in an environment where less than 20% of us work out. Do you?

Second Theme:
Openness to Others and Greater Sensitivity to "Socio-Eco-Civic" issues

The trend toward Social Withdrawal that gathered momentum from 1996 to 2002 was reversed in 2003. We are now witnessing a new "Need for Proximity." People are expressing a renewed desire to reach out and be connected with the people around them.

The first tangible indication of this attitude is the renewed importance of family. The notion of family, however, has widened dramatically to include unmarried couples, gay couples, close friends, and even professional colleagues.

The concept of family is changing from something that provides a comforting shelter in an uncertain world to an entity that provides the pleasure and stimulation to recharge our personal batteries. Increasingly, the family is a vehicle for personal projects both inside and outside the home.

Family is extending to Networking. People are seeking out others with whom they can create networks based on common values or interests. Increasingly, we are coming to the conclusion that life is a game best played with a wide circle of friends, acquaintances and colleagues.

We're becoming more aware of the people around us. We're realizing that exposing ourselves to the diverse realities of others will expand our own horizons. This desire to discover and explore new points of view carries with it a marvelous implication: our willingness to challenge and modify our convictions and beliefs is rising. And this kind of evolution contributes greatly to furthering Personal Growth.

The renewed celebration of diversity has led to what marketers are calling "Generation E.A.: Ethnically Ambiguous. The *New York Times* (12/2/03) reports that Ambiguity is chic, especially among the under-25 members of Generation Y, the most racially diverse population in the America's history. "Today what's ethnically neutral, diverse or ambiguous has tremendous appeal," says Ron Berger, The CEO of Euro RSCG MVBMS Partners, an advertising agency and trend research company whose clients include Polaroid and Yahoo. "Both in the mainstream and at the high end of the marketplace, what is perceived as good, desirable, successful is often a face whose heritage is hard to pin down." The increasingly multiracial American (and Canadian) population is due to intermarriage and waves of immigration.

"Some of us are just now beginning to recognize that many cultures and races are assimilating," says John Partilla, CEO of Brand Buzz, a marketing agency owned by the WPP group. "If what you're seeing now is our focus on trying to reflect the blending of individuals, it reflects a societal trend, not a marketing trend. For once, it's about art imitating life." Homogeneity, white bread, and vanilla are out. Fusion, mystery and hybrids are in.

The Need for Proximity is also expressed in greater community involvement. With our enhanced self-confidence and optimism, we're finding the emotional space to uplift the people around us. Our communities or causes have become a "second circle" in which we orbit. More and more of us want to give something back. Charity is good business.

Even the home "private bubble" is becoming more human. Cobi Ladner, editor of *House & Home*, states that people are beginning to react against clean urban modernism that can be "quite cold, bland verging on boring." She says, "People are not happy living in those spaces. From what I can see, I think things are starting to warm up again." We agree. From sea to shining sea, there's a new spirit of engagement. Optimism begins at home and spreads outwards.

We're also seeing renewed confidence in small business – both as suppliers of goods and services and potential places to build a career. They are perceived as enterprises that allow employees to express their creativity and individuality. In fact, even within large businesses, the trend is towards acting and thinking like a conglomeration of small businesses. It's all about the trend to caring and self-expression.

One of the most distinctive traits of sociocultural change in 2004 is the very clear penetration of values related to social conscience and ecology. After years of looking inward, people are not only more concerned about what's happening in their own backyard, they're willing to take both responsibility and action in favour of their community's welfare.

This "Socio-Eco-Civic" sensitivity is also showing itself in people's consumption behaviour. They're becoming more critical and selective. They're choosing products and services that respect social ethics. People are telling us that they are more willing to purchase products whose manufacture and use conform to a clear civic or eco-morality.

Third Theme:
Caution and Pragmatism in the face of Overload

While people are accepting "the certainty of uncertainty," they haven't yet embraced it fully. Despite the rise in self-belief and openness-to-others, people remain tired, wary and cautious. They're also still overwhelmed by the magnitude and multiplicity of challenges facing them.

Our increased confidence and hope has not translated into an increased appetite for risk. In fact, the trend to Risk Aversion increased strongly in 2003. We call this "Residual-Wariness." Our desire for fulfillment and achievement is growing but so is our allergy to the risk that accompanies bold endeavors.

A *Wall Street Journal*/NBC poll conducted at the beginning of March 2004 revealed that 47 per cent of those surveyed said they worried "America no longer has the same economic security it has had in the past."

People will therefore begin their initiatives with baby-steps. Inch by inch, they'll expose themselves to the peril of failure. Their burgeoning desire for autonomy is still fragile. One large blow could still send them back into their mental shelters.

"A decade of increasing demands from employers combined with conflicts between home and office has created a generation of frazzled Canadians who are booking more time off for mental and physical fatigue," says the *Globe and Mail* (10/22/03).

The biggest pressure is what Professor Linda Duxbury, of the University of Western Ontario, calls "Role Overload" – the feeling that there is not enough time available to meet the demands in one's professional and personal life. After surveying 31500 Canadians who work in public, private and non-profit organizations, Duxbury states that professional women reported working as hard as the men at work but also working harder than men at home. Dr. Brent Bost, a Texas based obstetrician and gynecologist, calls it "The Hurried Woman Syndrome" and he says it leads to an increase in anxiety and depression.

Duxbury's survey also found that 60 per cent of all respondents said they have trouble balancing their work and family demands and 28 per cent had missed at least three days of work in the past six months because of illness.

People are in search of ways to take back control of their life, hence the quest for tools of every kind to help them achieve more with less. From PDAs to power tools, they want easy-to-use instruments or technology that will increase their productivity while not interfering with their desire for simple and authentic pleasures.

Therefore we have higher expectations of the tools we buy. Their benefits must be immediately apparent. And their usefulness must make good on their promises.

The search for control is also the search for "More Time." With women assuming most of the responsibility for domestic chores, there has been a large shift towards "outsourcing" these services. In fact cleaning services have gone from being a discretionary luxury to an essential service. As the *National Post* (01/10/04) reports, "These days, most Canadians get their homes professionally cleaned every other week on average. With both partners in a typical couple working full time, workplace demands growing and commutes getting longer, families are keen to outsource household chores. An ageing population, well-heeled but less able to scour the sink, has also contributed to soaring demand. Even singles with busy careers are seeking household help." Four words would describe the trend in shopping habits over the next 24 to 36 months: **Forward To The Fundamentals**. People will express their pragmatism in their consumption behaviour. Frivolity is out. "Real Basic" is increasingly in.

So if you're marketing a product or service, highlight its real value-add while ensuring that it's not perceived as superfluous or merely ostentatious. Offer concrete solutions that meet fundamental needs. Establish your credibility through reliability, guarantees, efficiency and follow through.

Whatever it is that you're selling, your primary mandate is to help people come to terms with a life that is increasingly scary, overwhelming, risky and messy. On a rational level, your offering must offer best-in-class value-per-dollar. On an emotional level, it must stand for optimism, engagement, openness and integrity.

Now let's explore the Six Steps to acquiring *The Art of Personal Consistency – How To Always Play At Your Personal Best, When It Counts.*

LIVE IN THE
SWEET
SPOT.

STEP 1: Focus

Live In The Sweet Spot of What, Why and How.

Your "Focus" Self-Exploration

Here is a simple 10 point test to determine your command of this skill. For each question, rate yourself on a scale of 1-10.

- ☐ • I am very aware of the trends shaping my environment

- ☐ • I know the three specific goals I want to achieve in the next year

- ☐ • I communicate my goals clearly to my team-members

- ☐ • I am currently doing work I love to do

- ☐ • I know what my unique talent is

- ☐ • I am fully using my unique talent at work

- ☐ • I know the main benefit I deliver to other people

- ☐ • I have a clearly defined personal strategy to achieve my desired goals

- ☐ • I feel like I'm in control of my own destiny

- ☐ • I would call myself a happy person

◯ total

- **If you scored between 85 and 100**
Congratulations. You're already Focused.
- **If you scored between 70 and 84**
You're almost there - you just need a little more vision and concentration.
- **If you scored less than 70**
Your life is still a blur.
This chapter will help you clarify what's important to you so you can take action to achieve it.

Let's dialogue for a minute. If I told you that Helen is a focused person, what qualities would you immediately associate with her, even if you knew nothing else about her? Determined? Forceful? Results oriented? Not prone to distraction? Clearheaded? Sharp? No-nonsense? Do you agree? What other qualities can you think of?

On the other hand, if I told you that Helen was an unfocused person, what would you think of her? Confused? Ineffective? Stressed? Messy? Vague? Absent minded? Forgetful? Erratic? Frustrated? Anxious? Anything else?

How would people describe you? How focused do you appear to the people around you? More importantly, how focused do *you* believe you are? The Self-Exploration on the previous page will have given you some idea. But here's the brutal truth about focus: it's an all-or-nothing thing. You can't be kind-of, semi, quasi, sort-of, somewhat focused. You are or you aren't.

Focus is the gateway to Personal Consistency. It's the Abracadabra that makes the magic of being On-Fire possible. Without it, life is a hit-or-miss exercise. If you don't know precisely what you want, how can you achieve it?

Social psychologist, Barry Schwartz claims in his new book, *The Paradox of Choice: Why More is Less*, that what's making so many people unhappy is that, unlike previous generations, we have too many choices – not just at the supermarket, but in our jobs, in where we live, and with whom. Like any feast, if you cannot decide what you want, you'll either starve or gorge yourself into sickness. Only by focusing on what feeds us at the deepest level, can we grow and prosper.

The great Performance-Paradox:

The vast majority of my Clients know exactly what they want to achieve for their business or their employers but they don't know what they want for *themselves*.

They have their budgets, their targets and their quotas. They have their external benchmarks that tell them how they're doing daily, weekly or monthly, but they don't have their inner guides to direct their everyday thoughts, actions and emotions.

In fact, over ninety per cent of the clients I work with, haven't clearly defined what they should be focused on. They don't have a precise understanding of *What* they want to achieve, *Why* they want to achieve it, and *How* they're going to achieve both their *What* and their *Why*.

Don't get me wrong. They sort of know what they want to achieve, they kind of know why they're doing what they're doing and they have a general idea of how to achieve it. Relative to the general population, my Clients are highly successful people. But when they're pressed to clearly articulate their personal *What, Why* and *How*, they struggle. The knowledge may be there but it hasn't been brought to their conscious surface. For the most part, they're acting instinctively.

How about you? Right here, right now, in two minutes or less, could you tell me your *What, Why* and *How* in such a way that by the end of the allotted 120 seconds, both you and I would be motivated to achieve all three?

If you cannot, the odds of you catching fire are a matter of chance. As Shakespeare wrote, "Be not afraid of greatness. Some are born great. Some achieve greatness and some have greatness thrust upon them." If you're born great, you may not need to read any further. If greatness is thrust upon you, Focus may be superfluous. However, if you want to achieve greatness, you're going to have to get focused fast.

Why the urgency? Because your job is in jeopardy, your clients are desperately seeking an edge (or a price-cut that you can't afford) and your peers/competitors are becoming better by the day.

According to the *Wall Street Journal* (11/7/03), "As the U.S. enjoys explosive growth in productivity, the effects are reaching into far corners of the economy. Once confined to the computer sector, productivity gains have spread into the vast service sector. Strong productivity growth means companies are producing more with less, which helps to explain why millions have been locked out of the job market even as the economy recovers."

Think for a moment: in the past year, have you experienced explosive growth in personal productivity? Are you demonstrably more effective today than you were twelve months ago? Six months ago? Three months ago? If you're not, you're lagging your environment.

Do you have "Bilateral Awareness"?

Those who are unaware are unaware that they're unaware. If you're not conscious of what you need to do, you won't do it. It's not on your mental radar. You won't take simple actions that could make the difference between success and failure. I see it all the time: people berating themselves for not doing the "small stuff" that could have delivered the results they craved. Anything is obvious once it's been thought of. **"If Only" is the battle cry of those who suffer from the benefit of hindsight but remain forwardly myopic.**

The person with the highest level of *Bilateral Awareness* wins. That means awareness of what's going on both inside of you and around you. It's a conscious recognition of what you want to achieve for yourself in the context of where the environment is headed.

For example, I want to become one of North America's top ten motivators in the next twelve months. That means I have to deliver 170 sessions with evaluations that are rated "outstanding" over 90 per cent of the time. I have to achieve this objective in an environment that is increasingly optimistic but still highly fearful. People want to believe their life is improving. They're looking for the signs. But they've been through too much to lose sight of the bogeymen and pitfalls that could trip them up at any moment. I have to design my content and delivery accordingly.

This book is a direct expression of my Bilateral Awareness. I'm writing it for three primary reasons. Firstly, to clarify and codify my own philosophy. Secondly, to help you do the same with your philosophy. Thirdly, it's what I do. It's my calling. It's how I stay relevant so that people continue to want to hear my message.

Without Bilateral Awareness you'll succumb to the "noise" of everyday life. As Kristin van Ogtop, the managing editor of *Real Simple* magazine, said, "We have noise from the minute we wake up in the morning to the minute we go to bed." According to the *New York Times* (03/21/04), *Real Simple* magazine has built its readership over the past four years – circulation has grown from 400 000 to 1.55 million – largely on people's desire to filter that noise.

Through knowing what to look for and what to ignore, Bilateral Awareness will help you process the world through the most effective filter for you. And by the way, that's how I selected the articles to be featured in this book. I scanned 1200 newspapers over about 55 weeks. The search for information on Personal Consistency was my filter. Without it, the information would have just been a blur.

How are you expressing your Bilateral Awareness? What's your filter? What's your Personal Operating Philosophy? What are the key environmental vectors reshaping your future? What actions are you taking to take charge of your life? How are you going to win? And how are you going to help others do the same?

If you want to realize your dreams, wake up! And this is a wake-up call of the best kind.

If you're a little concerned right now, that's my objective. I've got you focused on enhancing your Personal Productivity. You're about to take significant action before a real outside crisis forces you to. You're being proactive. You're ahead of the curve just when you thought you were behind the eight ball. Congratulations! Now for the next exhilarating step. It's time to define your unique *What, Why* and *How.*

Of all the actions I'll request you to take in this book, this may be the most important. It's about kindling the fire within you to light your path in the wild and weird times ahead. Without it, you're going to get lost, stressed-to-death or left behind. Guaranteed.

Despite my personal branding as "One of the world's leading Social Guides," I'm not sure I know any more than you what the future holds. As the saying goes, if you want to make God laugh, show him your plans. But what I do know is this: you and I ain't seen nothing yet. The change that has brought us to this point is eminently mild compared to what's coming.

As the *New York Times* (7/31/03) article on Microsoft stated: "The recent organizational maneuvers are the preparations of an ambitious company on the cusp of a new cycle of opportunity and growth. The changes in how people work, play and communicate are really just beginning. "Our innovation challenge is that there's this big opportunity to change many things," says Bill Gates, Microsoft's Chairman. "The actual achievement of software in delivering benefits to customers is, say, 20 per cent of what it will be even by the end of this decade."

Only Microsoft, Mr. Gates says, has the skills, money and Focus to put all the software pieces together – a concept the company calls 'integrated innovation' – to deliver the promise of the digital world, at low cost, to hundreds of millions of people and hundreds of thousands of companies. It's a bold vision, and an inspiring one to those toiling at Microsoft's sprawling corporate campus outside Seattle."

When it comes to change, what's good for Bill Gates and Microsoft is good for you and me. In your and my micro-universes, we can dominate. We're all "on the cusp of a new cycle of opportunity and growth." But only those of us who harness our personal power through a consciously compelling *What*, *Why* and *How* will prevail.

"Consciously Compelling"

What does this phrase mean to you? Before you go any further, think about it.

To me, it means the difference between inertia and breakthrough. It means being acutely aware of something that I find highly energizing. It means having a Mental Accelerator that drives my thoughts and actions in all circumstances, especially those that are most likely to distract me. It means being continually cognizant of something that excites me at a primal level.

I'll tell you something: I've coached people who were operating on automatic pilot. They were stuck in a rut. They had lost their spirit. Their fires had dwindled to weakly glowing embers. They were merely going through the motions. **Simply by get-**

ting them to articulate a consciously compelling goal, purpose and strategy in their own words, I helped them catch fire again. They knew what, why and how to do what they had to do, they just didn't know they knew.

I'll share this with you: whenever you see someone in love with what they're doing, you're looking at someone who has a consciously compelling *What*, *Why* or *How*. Put this point to the test. The next time you meet a Person-On-Fire, ask them why they're so hot. You'll hear an impassioned description of what compels them to perform at the deepest level.

I know you're hot (or at least very warm) otherwise you wouldn't even have got this far. What consciously compels you? Tell me in 50 words or less by e-mailing me at mike.lipkin@environics.ca.

Let's now explore the *What*, *Why* and *How* of Personal Consistency.

"What"
Your-Consciously-Compelling-Personal-Outcome. The Main Thing is to keep The Main Thing The Main Thing.
If your Personal Success is a target, think of Your-Consciously-Compelling-Personal-Outcome as the bulls-eye. It's the specific, measurable, inspirational result you want to achieve within a clearly defined timeframe. It's a result that will stretch, excite and delight you. It's an achievement that will make you proud of being You. It's your Personal Super Bowl, Stanley Cup or World Series. It's an external objective, visible to all. Or it's a deeply private goal that only you can see.

Do you have one? Two? Three?

By definition, without Your-Consciously-Compelling-Personal-Outcome, you cannot be focused. You cannot achieve Personal Consistency. And you sure as heck will not always perform at Your-Personal-Best when it counts.

So right now, write down one to three outcomes you would dearly love to achieve in the next twelve months.

Write down one to three outcomes you would love to achieve in the next month.

Write down one to three outcomes you want to achieve in the next week.

Write down one outcome you want to achieve before you go to sleep.

Think of your next meeting and write down the most important outcome you want to achieve through it.

Become Outcome-Centric. You know why? Because everything is created twice: first in the mind, then in reality. Freud called what happened in the mind *Primary Logic*. He called what happened in reality *Secondary Logic*. The one is a direct consequence of the other. If you see it in your mind's eye, your odds of creating it in reality are exponentially greater. "*First I throw my mind over the bar,*" said Dick Fosbury, the legendary high jumper and inventor of the Fosbury-Flop, "*and then my body follows.*"

As I'm writing these words, I'm seeing *On Fire* coming off the presses on July 1, 2004. I can feel the book in my hands. I'm experiencing an awesome thrill. By December 2004, I've seen my book in 20 000 homes and offices across the U.S. and Canada. I've seen myself delivering 170 seminars based on *On Fire* before the end of 2005. I've read the rave reviews. I've received e-mails from the thousands of people who've taken themselves to the next level because of it. All of these things have already happened. I'm in lag time. The actual occurrence of these things in reality is a mere formality.

What makes this process so powerful for me is not the book sales or number of seminars, it's the emotions that accompanies these achievements. I'm addicted to the feelings of achievement, fulfillment, pride, acknowledgement, wonder, growth, connection, kudos, adventure and excitement. By focusing on experiencing these feelings in advance, I experience them in advance – with all the energy and drive that comes with them.

This is not just a Mike Lipkin Rant. I've been through this process twice before – with my two previous books – *Your Personal Best* and *Luck Favours The Brave*. On both occasions, my vision translated into the precise results I aspired to achieving.

Why am I telling you this? Because **having a Consciously-Compelling-Personal-Outcome is a lightning rod for Confidence, the invincible belief in your own ability.**

Then, once you achieve your Outcome, your Confidence levels skyrocket. Doubt dwindles. And you attract even more success and luck. It's called Momentum and the more of it you have, the more irresistible you become.

By the way, there is also high tech help at hand. For just $5.95 a month or $49.95 a year, Mygoals.com will send you unlimited e-mail reminders to stick to your guns.

Interdependence Gives You Wings.

As you craft Your-Consciously-Compelling-Personal-Outcome, make sure it enhances the well-being of the people around you. You won't attract the favours of your Fellow Angels unless your desired outcomes help them achieve theirs.

All the People-On-Fire I know who have consistently achieved huge outcomes have greatly benefited the people around them. It's called the Law of Reciprocity: the more you help others, the more they want to help you. Not only that, every time you help someone else, your self-image as a coach, mentor or giver is reinforced. Your energy levels are augmented and your feelings of abundance beget more abundance. It's a beautiful thing.

In my case, I'll talk to approximately 100 000 people live. That means direct contact with 100 000 families. Then my books and CDs will touch at least another 100 000 people. And what this means is that I will influence about a million people in the next twelve months. Wouldn't that excite you? It thrills me. It's about as close to Nirvana as I'm going to come. What's your Nirvana? How are you going to get there?

If you're a leader, ensure everyone is part of a Consciously-Compelling-Team-Outcome

Based on all my work with teams in hundreds of companies across North America, the primary hallmark of good leaders is their simple willingness to invest the time to ensure their people understand a Consciously-Compelling-Team-Outcome. They believe it's important and they let their people know it's important.

As far as they can, they communicate the Consciously-Compelling-Team-Outcome to their people. The good leaders communicate the Consciously-Compelling-Team-Outcome in way that their people understand it. The great leaders communicate it in a way that their people want to achieve it. The difference between the two is reflected in the marketplace.

In fact, a Consciously-Compelling-Team-Outcome is often the difference between kicking ass and being ass-kicked. When the rubber meets the road, the power of motivation and morale kicks in. In a "More-with-less" environment, people's minds will take them so far. It's their hearts that take them the rest of the way.

It's people's immediate leader who determines their level of motivation. If you have even one person reporting to you, you have to ensure he wholeheartedly buys into the Consciously-Compelling-Team-Outcome.

I see it all the time within North America's top companies — even within the same zip code. One team-leader fires up her people with goals that capture their imagination. Another stays overly task-focused. It's a no-contest. The team with fired-up people triumphs every time.

So what's your Consciously-Compelling-Team-Outcome? How clear is it? How motivational is it? Whatever your response, take it to the next level.

And, by the way, if you feel your leader is not communicating the Consciously-Compelling-Team-Outcome with you, speak up. **In an increasingly web-enabled, matrix, fluid corporate environment, fortune favours the vocal ones. You get what you communicate.**

The alternative is to remain silent and stew in your own juices of resentment, frustration and self-pity. The difference is that dramatic. I talk every day with both kinds of employees: the bold and the beleaguered.

In an interview with the *Financial Times* (11/20/03), Carly Fiorina, Chairman and CEO of Hewlett-Packard and architect of the $19 billion merger with Compaq, spoke about the power of a Consciously-Compelling-Team-Outcome: "I tell people inside HP that leadership requires a strong internal compass. A company can get thrown off course if it isn't clear about its goals. It can get thrown off its moorings in terms of ethics and standards if it is tempted by the wrong things. A person can get buffeted by conventional wisdom that is frequently wrong. So you have to learn to ignore a lot of conventional wisdom and a lot of talk that isn't core to the purpose of what you're doing. I knew what we were doing was right for the company. Therefore I had no alternative but to keep doing it."

Remember, staying connected to a Consciously-Compelling-Team-Outcome will get you through short-term frustrations and slowdowns. As an outstanding coach, captain or player, your role is keeping your colleagues' eyes on the end-zone at all times. Be the one who keeps realigning the team to the Main Thing.

"Why"
Your-Burning-Personal-Passion. It's about the Intersection of the Triumphant Triad: Love, Cause, and Unique-Talent

"He who knows the "why" for his existence will be able to bear almost any 'how'."
Viktor Frankl

It's Monday morning. You think about the week ahead. You think of your challenges, your opportunities, your roadblocks, your allies, your competitors, your colleagues, your adversaries and your hassles.

Are you excited? Do you sizzle with anticipation? What sparks the fire-in-your-belly? What makes you best-in-class? What's your empowering cause? What calls you to action with a voice that cannot be denied? What's your "Why"?

A powerful "Why" lives in the Sweet-Spot where Love, Cause and Unique-Talent intersect.

"Love"

"Love" means doing something because it thrills you. It means being willing to do for free what others would pay you to do. It means relishing every opportunity to do more of it. It means sustaining your passion even during those moments when things go horribly wrong. It means doing something you believe you're genetically wired to do.

If you don't have a *Love* this thrilling or intense, welcome to the visible majority. People fired up with *Love* are a rarity. That's why those who have it shine so brightly. If, as you read these words, you're not fuelled by a *Love*, begin thinking about what it could be. Ask your Higher Source of Inspiration, whomever that may be, to guide you. Remember, if you ask the right questions, you'll get the right answers. Maybe they'll come soon and maybe you'll have to wait awhile. But delays are not denials. Sometimes, you have to slow down to hurry up.

"I love what I do," says Eddie Greenspan, Canada's top criminal lawyer who believes his 35-year career has surpassed his wildest dreams, "I haven't lost a bit of interest, enthusiasm or energy. I love fighting for people. I love fighting the State. I wake up every morning and I can't believe I'm a lawyer." Determined not to coast, Greenspan, 60, still camps in his office, in a beautiful, restored bank building in downtown Toronto, six days a week and logs well over 60 hours of work. His case preparation is unflagging, as is his commitment to spreading the gospel of defense advocacy. Ask him what drives him and he will say a pure love of the law (*Globe and Mail* 11/29/03).

If like Eddie Greenspan, you have a big enough *Love*, you'll find a way to become a Person-On-Fire. I see it in the eyes of People-On-Fire. It's a perennial incandescence that grows stronger with time. They're passionate about what they do and it shows.

For me it's simple: I love to talk. I love sharing my insights with people. I love the interaction. I love the laughter. I love the energy. And yes, I love the applause and the kudos that comes with every great presentation.

I grew up with a stutter. While it never prevented me from talking up, it made talking in front of people a threatening experience. I always lived in anticipation of the verbal block that would publicly embarrass me. While my stutter grew milder over the years, it never left me. Until I decided I wanted to become a public speaker.

In 1991, I went through a year of severe depression. After a series of treatments that included psychotherapy, drug therapy, hospitalization and electro-convulsive therapy, I regained my joie de vivre. Shortly after my recovery, I wrote an account of my struggle for a South African magazine. Fortuitously, in the same month my story appeared, so did an article on professional speakers and the agents who represented them.

I contacted one of the agents who were featured. I convinced her I had a story that her Clients would find compelling. She agreed to represent me and she booked me my first speaking engagement, which she attended.

After the engagement, she told me calmly that she was terminating our agreement. "You want to be a professional speaker and yet you stutter," she said. "That's like wanting to be an athlete with a limp. It's a pity. You've got great presence. You've got a great message. But when you stutter, you make the audience feel uncomfortable. I'm sorry."

As I saw my dream drift away, I asked her for one last chance. I promised her I would never again stutter in front of an audience. I guaranteed her I could control my fluency with the right amount of concentration. I persuaded her that it was more the "first talk jitters" than a chronic defect. With all the passion I could muster, I begged her for an encore. After a long hesitation, she agreed.

As someone once said to me, "Nothing crystallizes the mind like the lack of an alternative." I knew that stuttering was not an option. I rehearsed. I concentrated. I immersed myself in images of pleasure and fulfillment as a future world-class speaker. I psyched myself with a pre-talk ritual that continues to this day. And I never stuttered on stage again.

Off stage, it's a different story. Paradoxically, when I'm relaxed, I stutter. I don't have to concentrate as hard. And so, stuttering has become a luxury for me that I can only afford when I'm with friends and family who accept me just the way I am.

Why am I telling you all of this? Because as the saying goes, *Love* conquers all. **If you have a deep enough desire to do something, you'll find a** way or make a way. **What's more, if you demonstrate courage and commitment to your passion, life conspires with you to make it happen.** There is no such thing as a hopeless situation, there are just people who become hopeless about the situation. Find a way or make a way.

"Cause"
"Great minds have purposes, others have wishes."
Washington Irving

"*Cause*" is the contribution you want to make to others. It's the difference you want to make in their lives. It's the value you want to add to them because it will enrich both your life and theirs. It's something so valuable to you that you're willing to invest whatever it takes to achieve it – money, time and emotion.

If you don't have a *Cause*, you can't have the Fire. It's the *Cause* that imbues you with the authenticity and authority that attracts others to you. Ironically, it's only when you're motivated to benefit others that you truly benefit yourself.

You and I both know people who are motivated purely by personal gain. We hear their promises and their reassurances but we know better. Maybe we trusted them once. Over time, though, they revealed their self-centredness and we withdrew our commitment to them.

In People-On-Fire, there is a direct correlation between their passion and the contribution they want to make to others. They live to make a difference. They are the rebels with a *Cause*. Peter Gabriel, the legendary musician whose solo career spans 28 years, is such a creature. In 1982, he established Womad (world of music and dance), gathering together artists from all over the world to perform at festivals. To date, there have been Womad festivals in 70 countries. He also launched a Record label, Real World, to sign up the artists coming over to Womad who couldn't get signed anywhere else.

In an interview with the *National Post* (11/10/03) he states, "Music is central to my existence. I get excited by ideas, and I really enjoy collaborating with people who have more talent, smarts or skills than me, because I learn something every time. But if I go too long without making music, I'm like a junkie in need of a fix. After a few days, I'm walking around with my tongue hanging out, looking for a piano." What's your Benign-Narcotic?

From 53-year-old Peter Gabriel to 12-year-old Ryan Hreljac. As reported by the *Globe and Mail* (11/18/03), Ryan is a seventh grader from Kemptville, a small town in Ontario,

Canada. He has raised $800 000 to build 70 wells since he was six and learned that people in Africa were dying of contaminated water. He has been featured on Oprah, honoured by Governor General Adrienne Clarkson and received communion from Pope John Paul in Rome. He is also the 2003 winner of the World of Children Founder's Award, a US$15 000 scholarship announced at the United Nations in New York on November 18, 2003.

He got the idea of funding a well in Africa in Grade 1. He asked his parents for money by doing extra chores, then hit up his classmates, friends and neighbours. His charitable work has since taken him to schools and conferences in China, Japan, Australia, Italy and the U.S.

One of the people whom he helped was Jimmy Akana, a 10-year-old boy from a village in Uganda. Jimmy and Ryan became pen pals. After becoming a refugee, Jimmy was adopted by the Hreljac family. Today, Ryan and Jimmy live under the same roof.

For *Sesame Street*, now into its 35th year, the cause according to executive producer, Lewis Bernstein, is "To influence kids at an early age and give them the skills they need to navigate their way through school and in life." In an interview with the *Toronto Star* (04/03/04), Bernstein states, "When I first came here (in 1972) there were a lot of ex-hippies working here with a spirit of Let's Change The World. Maybe some of us have cut our hair, but the passion hasn't changed. Life doesn't exist in most places like it does on *Sesame Street* but if we don't model it, it'll never exist."

On scales both big and small, having a *Cause* is the key to extraordinary achievements. If you're without a cause, find one. It needs to be in alignment with your *Love* and your *Unique-Talent*. Begin it now. You never know where it may lead you.

My *Cause* can be described in five words: "I excite people into action." I want to motivate people to do what they otherwise would not have done to get the results they otherwise would not have gotten.

I want to help everyone stay On Fire in the face of continuing challenges. I want to help them segue from 'Lives of Quiet Desperation' to 'Lives of Adventure, Accomplishment and Action'. So I go looking for opportunities to walk my talk in the subway, the marketplace and the community. And here's a truth: whatever you look for, that's what you find. So the more I look for ways to guide others, the more ways I find. How are you enhancing your capacity by enhancing the capacity of the people around you?

Seize every opportunity to strengthen the *Why* that drives you at the deepest level. The more you practice, the better you become. When I practice motivating people, I may or may not be receiving a fee. The real reward to me is never the money. It's the expansion of my power-to-motivate, my enhanced capacity after the event.

Every act is a cause set in motion. Get good by doing good. This is not charity; it's fundamental to staying On Fire. We become what we repeatedly do. Our acts become our habits. Our habits become our character. Our character becomes our destiny. So don't just give because it's the right thing to do. Give because it's the selfish thing to do. It's the optimal way to use your talents more of the time. And the more you use your talents, the better you'll be. And the more people you'll impact and the more prosperous and powerful you'll become.

"Unique-Talent"

"She speaks 3-year-old" is how the *New York Times* (01/04/04) describes 65-year-old Anne Wood's *Unique-Talent*. Anne Wood is the developer of *Teletubbies*, one of the most successful worldwide children's TV shows of all time. *Teletubbies* is now sold in 120 countries, including China and Russia. It has also made Anne Woods one of Britain's wealthiest women. Wood's collaborator, Andrew Davenport, says she has the ability to see things "from the persona of a child. She knows exactly the point at which a child will get confused. She's actually able to see it from the point of view of a 3-year-old."

Jay Leno was branded by *Fortune* magazine as 'The MVP of Late Night TV. His *Unique Talent*, according to *Fortune* (2/23/04), is "to pick over jokes, news items, and tidbits of information – he gets 200 to 300 submissions a day – select the funniest of the crop, and fashion them into an 11 minute monologue that will persuade millions of Americans to stay up later than they probably should for a humorous take on the events of the day."

What's your *Unique-Talent*? What's your Michelangelo, Einstein, Picasso or Gretzky? I know you have one. Everyone has. But if you cannot articulate it clearly, you're part of the 99 per cent of people who live in ignorance of their greatest asset – their potential engine of extraordinary personal success.

Seriously, when I question people in my seminars about their personal genius, they look around uncomfortably, fidget with their fingers and respond with a tepid "I suppose it could be..." or "I think I'm quite good at..." or "My main strength is probably..."

After talking to more than a million people in twenty countries over eleven years, I know that **People-On-Fire have a very clear sense of their Unique-Talent. They know they have to be excellent at a range of tasks but they can only be a Genius at one of them.**

For Anne Wood, it's understanding 3-year-olds. For Steve Jobs, it's making complex technology simple and alluring to individuals. For Nelson Mandela, it's helping others see the good in everything and everybody. For Jim Carrey, it's the ability to contort his face into impossible but comic dimensions. For Roger Clemens, it's the ability to pitch a 96 mile-an-hour fastball into the strike zone. For Mike Lipkin, it's the ability to excite people instantly through the written and spoken word. For you, it's _____?

Instinctively, we all know what our *Unique-Talent* is. We just haven't invested either the time or the effort in clearly defining it.

Think about what you're awesome at.
Think about your special strength.
Think about your natural aptitude.
Think about what comes easier to you.
Think about what activity puts you "in the zone."
Think about the thing you do effortlessly that so many others struggle with.
Think about what gives you a natural high and sense of fulfillment.

If you think about it, it will come. When it does, describe it to yourself and others in such a way that everyone is excited by it. Don't short-change yourself. Your *Unique-Talent* is a huge thing both to you and the people you serve. It's the difference between a life lived to the full and a life not lived at all.

In 1906, Vilfredo Pareto, an Italian economist, noted that eighty percent of Italy's wealth was concentrated in about twenty percent of the population. Later, this discovery became known as Pareto's Law – "the vital few and the trivial many". The vital 20 per cent of people or tasks created 80 per cent of the results, while the trivial 80 per cent of people or tasks created 20 per cent of the results.

Well, in 2004, Mike Lipkin, the Canadian Motivator, introduces the 99:1 Law:
Ninety Nine per cent of the true breakthroughs are created by One per cent of the population. In companies, communities and countries, it's the Outstanding One Per Cent that make it possible for the remaining ninety-nine percent to move forward.

The "One Percent" are people with a pronounced sense of their *Unique Talent*. They also have the confidence and the determination to apply it. Do you? If you do nothing else as a result of this book, identify your *Unique-Talent*. Then do whatever it takes to apply and develop it.

Become a *One Percenter* not just because it's your fast-track to the stars. Become a One Percenter so you can inspire others to do the same. Bring together your *Love, Cause* and *Unique-Talent* and you'll live in the Sweet Spot of personal alignment.

It was Milton who said: a man can make a Heaven of any Hell or a Hell of any Heaven. I believe that if you live your *Love, Cause* and *Unique-Talent*, you'll find your Personal Heaven, irrespective of circumstances. If you don't, no matter how sweet your environment, true fulfillment will always elude you. Think about how many people you know who appear to have it all, yet they act as if they have nothing. At their core, there's an empty spot, not the sweet spot. What about you? Did these comments hit the spot? Or did they hit a nerve?

Here's Lipkin's Personal Power Paradox: your greatest strength is always your greatest weakness but the power of your strength vastly overcompensates for your weakness.

At a recent seminar with a large advertising agency, one of the copywriters in the audience told me that she believed her greatest weakness was her tendency to keep over-analyzing and dissecting whatever anyone said to her. As a result, she told me that she lived in a state of continual mistrust and suspicion of others. I asked the CEO of the company whether this woman was excellent at what she did. "The best!!" he replied unequivocally.

So I asked her what she believed made her such a great copywriter. "My ability to dissect human emotions and express the heart of the real issues." I then asked her whether she would be prepared to lose her strength in order to lose her tendency to over-analyze the responses of others. Shaking her head, I could see that she got it immediately. In fact, I think she probably even made friends with her perceived weakness because she now clearly understood the power it gave her.

My greatest strength is the ability to get excited about anything. I can go from ennui to excitement in a nanosecond. What's more, my enthusiasm is highly contagious. Within moments, I can harness other people's energy to my cause. So what's the downside? Well, I tend to dare where angels fear to tread. As a result, I've stepped on a few landmines that more cautious, sedate souls may have avoided. I've said things I shouldn't have said. I've made enemies I shouldn't have made. I've lost revenue and resources I shouldn't have lost.

But you know what? Whatever the mistakes I've made, they're nothing compared to the joy and fulfillment I've received from my excitement. If you think about your greatest strengths and weaknesses, I'm sure you'll reach the same conclusion.

And you know what else? I've even stopped trying to correct my weaknesses. I'm aware of them. I've surrounded myself with people whose strengths neutralize them. I avoid assignments that require them. But I choose to invest my time heightening my strengths not becoming less weak at my limitations. It's also a heck of a lot more fun to become more of a Picasso than it is to become less of a dunce.

"How"

Translating Passion into Results Through Your Hot-Personal-Strategy

"O Lord, grant me the freedom of a tightly defined strategy." David Ogilvy, founder of the Ogilvy & Mather Advertising Agency

Chances are, if you're reading these words, you're one of the more than 60 per cent of North Americans over 30. You're also one of the more successful residents of this continent. I know this because my readers tend to lead the pack. That's why they read my work – to sharpen their edge so they can take themselves to the next level.

After that little bit of stroking, here are three tough questions:

What's your Proprietary Plan for achieving your Outcome and Passion?
In 50 words or less, how would you describe the rationale supporting the way you behave during the 40 to 60 hours you spend at work every week?
In 50 words or less, how would you describe your strategy for overall success, happiness and well-being?

In other words, I'm asking you to articulate *How* you'll achieve your *What* and *Why*.

The *Webster's Dictionary* defines Strategy simply as: *a method for obtaining a specific result.* I can't put it any more succinctly than that. So what's your distinctive method for achieving a specific result? What's your discipline for achieving your desired outcome? What's your rudder that keeps you sailing in the right direction during tumultuous times?

Do you have one? You've probably been on the planet for over thirty years. In all that time, I know you've taken a few hours to fine-tune your Personal Strategy? Or maybe not.

Once again, here's the Truly Great Human Mystery: why do so few people do the simple things that deliver the results so many people crave? Is it because they haven't had this BFO – Blinding Flash of the Obvious? Or is it because they don't believe it can be this easy? Or could it be that they're afraid of living La Vita Maxima?

Answer: all of the above, to a greater or lesser degree. **There is a price to be paid for living in the Self-Actualization zone. It's the relentless challenge of personal change and reinvention. It's the lack of cruise control. It's the Personal Dare that one sets oneself every day. It's a way of life that paves the way for others to follow.** It's the Way of the One Percenter.

The reason that I pursue the **What, Why** and **How** of Personal Consistency is that the alternative is too horrible to contemplate. I live in fear of chanting Marlon Brando's classic lament in his role as Terry Malloy in *On the Waterfront*: "I coulda had class. I coulda been a contender. I coulda been a somebody."

If not now, then when? If not you, then who? Nothing is as excruciating as the pain of regret. On planet Earth, you cannot go back. So go forward. Distill your Hot-Personal-Strategy for success.

Plant these questions in your mind to incubate a direction for yourself over time:

What is the best way to leverage my passion, cause and unique talent to achieve my compelling outcome?
What is the best way to differentiate myself from the people around me so I stand out?
What are the most powerful actions that will maximize the impact of my resources and energy in my quest for my compelling outcome?
What approach can I take that will become more effective over time?
What strategy feels best to me?
How can I merchandize my strategy to others in such a way that I attract them to my cause?

A Hot-Personal-Strategy is like an all-purpose-vehicle for your life.

Oscar Wilde, the great Victorian English playwright, once wrote a letter to a friend with the following opening line: "I was going to write you a shorter letter but I didn't have the time."

Attention spans, including yours, are short and they're getting shorter. A Hot-Personal-

Strategy Statement should be twelve words or less. Yup, in twelve words or less, how would you describe your Hot-Personal-Strategy? What is your rallying cry? What words are you using to enroll others' help in your personal quest?

Take out a pen and paper right now and have some fun. Off the top of your head, write down your Hot-Personal-Strategy Statement. Don't worry if it's right or wrong. Just write it. Write as many variations as you can. Then review them. Make them motivational, actionable, achievable, enjoyable, flexible, sustainable. Create one for your professional life and one for your personal life. Or create one that embraces both. There are no rules here. We're all making it up as we go along. I'm just a guy who may have some interesting perspectives for you because I spend my life with One Percenters. They walk this talk. And they get magnificent results.

I'm always amazed in my seminars how quickly people can express their Hot-Personal-Strategy with just a little coaching from me. It's like it has been living just below the surface, begging for a chance to break out. When it does, people are at first awestruck. Then they embrace it like an old friend. Only the vital few, however, stay the course and execute against it. The Doers are far outnumbered by the Talkers.

Here's what I do know: **if you have a Hot-Personal-Strategy that you live by, you have this thing called "Strategic Discipline." You have a way of buffering yourself against the negative and the non-essential.** You have a way of funneling your focus so you see the right things, extract the right meanings, make the right decisions and implement the right behaviours. A Hot-Personal-Strategy is like an all-purpose vehicle for your life. It will take you wherever you want to go, irrespective of circumstances.

I have two Hot Personal Strategies – one for my life as a whole and the other specifically for my career. As you'll see, they are entirely synergistic.

Lipkin's Life Strategy: Control of Destiny Through the Serious Pursuit of Good Luck

That's it. That's my method for achieving my desired results. I'm always focusing on Luck because I believe Luck stands for Love, Understanding, Courage and Knowledge. That's my Holy Grail, what's yours?

It's not important where you are right now. What's important is where you're going. Whatever you focus on, that's what you move towards. Focus is the great accelerator and magnifier.

I believe life is a mirror that reflects back at you what you are. Carry Love, Understanding, Courage and Knowledge within you and you become a magnet to everything that's associated with those four virtues.

My Life Hot-Personal-Strategy, therefore, is to consistently generate the right energy within me so I attract the right response from the outside world. Think about your life. Think about your great days. Think about your truly lousy days. Great days happen when you feel great. Lousy days happen when you feel lousy. The one is a direct function of the other.

The question is: what comes first? Does your internal energy create your external reality? Or does your external reality create your internal energy? Think about your answer carefully because your response will signal your status as a winner or a loser in the New Normal of the 2000s. Do not continue until you have decided what you believe.

Hmmm, if you believe that your internal energy creates your external environment, congratulations! You are fueled by the number one value of those people thriving on chaos, challenge and change: Control of Destiny.

At Environics/Lipkin, we define Control of Destiny as:

Total conviction that you're in charge of your own life; immunization against depression and despair; the attitude with which you accept those things that you cannot influence; investing all your energy in doing what's uniquely right for you; achieved through trial and error; your strongest source of personal power; the process by which you use each personal-win to prepare you for the next unprecedented crisis; aura of control and confidence which acts as a magnet to others; a personal code of conduct that sustains you in the tough moments and ensures you consistently deliver excellence; celebration of the struggle.

There is a Chinese fairy tale from Outer Mongolia that begins like all fairy tales: Once upon a time there was a humble shepherd who discovered an abandoned foal one day while he was tending his flock. Gently, carefully, he lifted the foal and took it home where he nurtured and raised it like a brother.

We can already tell what's going to happen in this fairy tale, right? The boy and the horse grow very close. As they both grow, the youth and the stallion become as one. Then the king stages the biggest horse race in the land. He offers his daughter's hand in marriage to the man who wins this horse race. The boy enters and wins.

So far, it's the classic Western fairy tale. But here, there's a sharp, clanging change, because the Chinese don't think the way we Westerners think. So when the boy comes to the King to claim his prize – the daughter's hand in marriage – the King screams at the boy: "Are you mad? How dare you assume I could ever give my daughter to a mere shepherd? You don't know her tastes! You don't know how she lives! She could never be your wife!"

All the noblemen and princes immediately chase the boy away in anger, hurling insults and shooting arrows at him as he flees. The horse is pierced a dozen times. When they get back to his cottage, the horse dies.

Now if this was a Western fairy tale, we know exactly what would happen. Good would prevail over evil. The boy would get what is rightfully his. He would have the King's daughter. Justice would win the day. The King would be punished. The noblemen and the princes who abused and cheated the boy would get their comeuppance.

But is that how life really works?

So that night, as the boy drifts into sleep, exhausted and heartbroken, the horse comes to him in a dream. "Before you bury me tomorrow," the horse says to the boy, "take my bones and sinews and make a harp to comfort yourself." The horse then goes on to describe in great detail which bones and sinews are to be selected and how the harp is to be made. Finally, in a farewell, the horse says to the boy: "Whenever you play this harp, you will be soothed and comforted and so will everyone who hears you."

What's the meaning of this fairy tale? **We all have a choice: we can get bitter or we can get better. It's entirely our call.** When life seems unfair, when injustice seems to have prevailed, we can choose to obsess on how we won the race and didn't win the prize. We can choose to blame and punish all those people who we think betrayed us. Or we can accept that we've just had a date with destiny; that we've just been through an experience that was waiting to happen.

Life is about crises. Some are big and some are small, but it's your ability to resolve them that ultimately determines whether you live at Your Personal Best. And the more successful you become, the more crises you will have.

The *Oxford Dictionary* defines a Crisis as "*a decisive moment; a turning point; a time of great difficulty.*" By definition, therefore, a life of great adventure, achievement and growth, is destined to be filled with crises. So savour them. Know that crises are merely milestones along the path of destiny. You control your destiny by the way in which you handle each crisis.

The moment you believe that you are in control of your own destiny, a magical thing will happen.

You will attract others to you. Let me ask you this question: in times of chaos and uncertainty, what do other people want most from you? Isn't it confidence? Isn't it a feeling of control? Isn't it a sense that if they go with you, they'll get what they want or they'll be secure. In times of great change and transformation, people crave security. It's our basic emotional need.

Through their actions, words and aura, the New Champions give others a sense of certainty. Think about the people who you're prepared to listen to and whom you respect. Don't they have an aura of control and confidence about them? Confidence is a magnet to others; it's the first thing that people search for in their leaders and team members.

The Virtuous Cycle

A Hot-Personal-Strategy is only as good as the efforts you make to apply it. **Strategy without the discipline of action is the beginning of delusion. Strategy is sculpted through execution. Every act validates or challenges the Strategy.**

Plan. Act. Evaluate. Change or Reinforce. Plan. Act. Evaluate. Change or Reinforce. Plan...It's the Virtuous Cycle. It's about acting with Strategic Awareness instead of operating on automatic pilot. If you're on a Virtuous Cycle, you're upward bound. All your experiences serve you because you're extracting the maximum meaning from them. You live life forwards because you understand it backwards.

Feedback is the breakfast of Champions. But what happens if you have no one to give you feedback? We're all the New Columbuses. No one knows what's uniquely right for you except you. We're all in search of undiscovered continents. You are your own best coach. So coach yourself. Be prepared for wins and losses. You cannot win if you're not prepared to lose. The secret is to use each loss as an opportunity to win more.

Here are the actions that comprise my Personal Code of Conduct. This is how I keep enhancing my Love, Understanding, Courage and Knowledge:

Every day, I go for the magic in each person I have the privilege to be with.
Every day, I expect more from myself, life and other people.
Every day, I help people control their destiny by connecting them with their unique personal power.
Every day, I play full out at whatever game I'm playing. I hold nothing back.

Every day, I feed my appetite for new ways to communicate and connect with people.
Every day, I condition my physical machine through the right food and exercise to perform at its peak.
Every day, I use words that inspire myself and others.
Every day, I go first. I lead by example.
Every day, I forgive myself for my mistakes so I can recover rapidly and start again.
Every day, I stay the course and raise my game when I am most fatigued.

Those are my personal standards. What are yours? Write them down now and keep them with you. Keep fine-tuning them until you've got a Personal Code of Conduct that sustains you in the tough moments and ensures you consistently deliver against your Hot-Personal-Strategy. This exercise is so important that I'd like you to e-mail your standards to me at mike.lipkin@environics.ca. I'll even give you feedback.

Weyerhaeuser Canada Ltd., a leading British Columbia based forest products company, has made Control of Destiny mandatory for all employees. To quote Mike Rushby, Vice President of Human Resources, "Every employee, every salaried employee, is required to have an individual development plan. Whether they are 20 years old or 60 years old, there is always an opportunity for growth and development."

Practice Control of Destiny Conditioning. Control of Destiny is a Life Tool that builds strength over time.

Like any other practice, Control of Destiny requires constant deposits of small and large triumphs before it becomes instinctual. So from now on, **every time you succeed at a challenging task, or achieve an extraordinary result in an extreme situation, take time to register the achievement at the deepest level. Imprint your personal power on your soul.** Then, take regular moments to recollect and celebrate your authority. It's called *Control of Destiny Conditioning*: the process by which you use each personal win to prepare yourself for the next unprecedented crisis.

Do you know why so few people really live an extraordinary life? Because most of us suffer from instant amnesia in the really, really tough moments. Most of us forget our moments of magnificence, probably because we didn't consider them to be magnificent in the first place. I see it all the time. I see people doubting themselves when they've come through far tougher challenges in their past. They fail to remember all the times they've surmounted the obstacles in front of them.

Have you noticed how many people will do anything for others? But when it comes to doing things for themselves, they are reticent. I'm not suggesting that you focus only on achieving your own Personal Best. I'm suggesting that you invest in the one resource that has the power to help you help so many other people: your control of the world around you based on your attitude towards it.

Try this: for the next ten minutes, think about those moments when you were spectacular. Think about when you exceeded not only your expectations but the expectations of all the people around you; think about your victories; think about your most courageous action; think about when you did the impossible; think about when you helped other people do the impossible; think about when you made yourself and your loved ones proud; think about when you felt really outstanding; think about when you absolutely refused to quit; think about when you faced down the odds and won. Think deeply. Think about ALL those moments, big or small. And make this a daily ritual. You will soon discover that your Control of Destiny Conditioning will manifest itself when you need it most.

I'll make a confession to you: often, when I'm about to present to very powerful, very wealthy, successful people, I experience a flash of terror. I think about how much they've achieved, what they know and how high their expectations are. On those occasions, I have to revisit previous presentations where I excelled in order to gather the courage and the self-belief to do it again. I continually dip into the best parts of my past to guarantee an outstanding future. On the other hand, I've made a point of forgetting those parts I don't wish to remember.

Lipkin's Career Strategy: Build Buzz by Consistently Spreading The Magic (I'm a Magician. What else can I do?)

Magic: any extraordinary or irresistible charm, influence or power. (*Webster's Dictionary*)

According to the famous psychiatrist, Carl Jung, there are four general *archetypes* that live within each one of us: the Sovereign, the Warrior, the Magician and the Lover. In Jungian psychology, an archetype is an inherited pattern of thought or symbolic imagery derived from the past collective experience and present in the individual unconscious. For the vast majority of us, probably including you, these archetypes exist unconsciously. That is, until now.

Let's explore the four archetypes and how they can help you:

The Sovereign stands tall. He looks people in the eye. He is very still. He is not aggressive; he doesn't throw his weight around. He doesn't have to, he knows his power. He is gentle.

The Warrior meets trouble head on. He is unafraid to face whatever challenges come his way. But he is not aggressive. Whereas the King stands still, the Warrior moves, he goes out to meet his challenge.

The Magician is intuitive, lateral thinking, a helper and a change agent. He reaches out. People talk to him. He is the Shaman or Wizard.

The Lover is not the testosterone-driven Don Juan. The Lover is highly sensitive. He reads people. He loves the act of loving. He supports and comforts. He loves to connect with others just for the pleasure of intimacy.

All of us have a dominant archetype that drives us. I'm a Magician. My wife, Hilary, is a Warrior. Many of my clients are Sovereigns. What are you?

As a Magician, my role is to transform people into the kind of people they can and want to be. I trade in dreams and desires. Through an irresistible charm, influence or power, I shift people's view of the world. Or I imbue them with certainty. Or I take away a wound or injury that impedes them. Or I reconnect them to their passion after years of pessimism.

Whatever I do, I have to do it with flair, imagination, inspiration, passion, confidence, knowledge, colour and grace. I have to evoke feelings of awe and amazement. Without the wonder, there can be no magic. Inertia can only be dislodged by a force greater than itself. The immovable object only becomes movable if the irresistible force cannot be resisted.

The more people I transform, the more they want to share their experience. They talk. They recommend. They refer me to their colleagues and peers. They become my advocates. My profile rises. I reach more people and the sequence of positive consequences never ends.

To keep the sequence surging forward, I have to deliver the "Oh My God" factor every time I'm on stage. One mediocre performance and my mystique melts away. I go from Magician to Mortal in a heartbeat. It happens sometimes and I hate it.

The opposite of Magic is Monotony, Boredom and Ordinariness — my three nemeses. My fear of them drives me almost as strongly as my love of Motivation, Transformation and Differentiation.

Everything I do is focused on the platinum goal: deliver a soul-stirring, life-changing, perspective-shifting experience to my audience that excites them into actions that get them results. The sights and sounds of my live performance have to break through their barriers to connect with them at a meaningful level. My written material must be bright and bold. My website must be colourful and comprehensive. In short, everything I do must be aimed at transcending the expected, sometimes by a lot, always by a little.

When it comes to building buzz, there's no difference between you, Hollywood or me. What do I mean? Even when films have a great opening weekend, they often collapse on the second weekend because of bad word of mouth. As Moritz Borman, CEO of International Media, stated in the *New York Times* (07/02/03), "You're not talking about a dumb herd of camels that you're trying to put into a theater. If you don't have a story, you don't have the word of mouth, and you don't have a second weekend."

So what's your story? What are you focused on? What strategy will catapult your career to the next level? What actions do you need to take consistently to bring your Strategy to life? How can you accelerate your Virtuous Cycle?

And, by the way, in a digital age, everything moves at the speed of Google. If you do something "brilliantly breakthrough," hundreds of thousands of people will find out about it at the press of a button. If you're just good or even excellent, no one cares. There are too many of those stories around. So use the new media. It can magnify your magic exponentially.

How Starbucks applies the *What, Why* and *How* to achieve global preeminence.

I don't know about you, but I'm a huge fan of Starbucks. I'm not sure I'd get through my weekdays without a hit of their Sumatra or Sulawesi. I've drunk Starbucks coffee in Toronto, New York, London and Shanghai. It's always good and it always gives me a lift.

But the real reason I'm a fan of Starbucks is the impact the company has made on my twenty-year-old daughter, Carla. She started working for Starbucks in April 2003, having just arrived in Canada from Johannesburg, South Africa. Like all new hires, she completed a five-day training program on how to become a Barista – "*someone who creates the Starbucks Experience for our customers by providing our customers with prompt service, quality beverages and products, and maintaining a clean and comfortable store environment.*"

Although she had never really worked before, within days Carla had embraced the Starbucks commitment to Legendary Service. Why? Because the folks at Starbucks got through to her like no one had ever done, including me. They gave her a meaningful What, Why and How. Then her supervisors modeled the behaviour they expected her to embrace. Her store manager and "Master Learning Coach" – Vik Sharma – consistently performed the "Values Walk" that defines the Starbucks way.

So, the Starbucks' *What* is: "To establish Starbucks as the premier purveyor of the finest coffee in the world while maintaining our uncompromising principles as we grow."

Their *Why* is: "To provide an uplifting experience that enriches people's daily lives."

Their *How* is: "Providing Legendary Service by creating meaningful experiences that inspire our customers to return more often and tell a friend."

If you talk to Carla or any one of the other tens of Baristas who are now her best friends, they will tell you very clearly how to apply the everyday small touches that bring their *What*, *Why* and *How* to life: learning customers' names and drink preferences, recognizing and acknowledging repeat customers, having personal interactions with customers, including customers in coffee tasting, responding appropriately when issues arise and assisting parents with children to a table.

Starbucks are also the masters of "Building Buzz." For example, on May 7, 2004, every Starbucks in North America offered a free Frappuccino to anyone who came into their stores. In addition to providing their customers with a hit of pleasure, Starbucks' objective was to get millions of people walking around with a Starbucks cup. At my local Starbucks in midtown Toronto, almost 2000 Frappucinos were served in a single day. That's Buzz-in-Action.

So, on a personal, micro level, could you articulate and execute your *What*, *Why* and *How* as powerfully as Starbucks? If you can, and you're truly committed to achieving them, you're on your way to your own unique Nirvana. If not, the best time to begin is now.

Here's Lipkin's Productivity Paradox: The harder you work, the less productive you become. And the converse? The happier you are, the more productive you become.

Environics' Social Values Research shows a marked rise in the number of people pursuing happiness in spite of the dictates of duty or work. They are reprioritizing the role of both work and money in their lives. They've discovered that if your job is a matter of life and death, you're going to be dead a lot. Instead, they are working to live.

Balance, or at least the desire for balance, is replacing sacrifice. As Michael J. Wolfe wrote in the *Entertainment Economy*, "From Real Goods to Feel Goods: If the eighties and nineties were about *I want my stuff*, the next decade will be about *I want to feel better, sexier, more informed, better fed and less stressed.*"

Increasingly, the leading adaptors are motivated to follow their own personal impulses before their obligations to others. They're not being selfish, they're being smart. They know that, while hard work never killed anyone, it certainly makes them stale and stagnant, especially if they're working hard at something they don't even love. That's called a living death. We've all been there. We've all felt that nauseous anxiety and tightness that accompanies tasks we hate doing. We've all felt the black weariness that hits us when we pass the point of diminishing mental returns. The best of us, however, know when to take a break before we snap.

The really productive people understand that stress erodes their personal effectiveness and blunts their edge. They know that they have no choice, so they do whatever it takes to boost their morale and happiness. Here's what I believe: **your happiness is not negotiable. If you're not happy, it's not possible for you to access your deepest resources. You'll always be looking over the fence at the grass that's greener on the other side.**

In my seminars, I often tell audiences that I'm not doing it for the money. I tell them I'm doing it for the love. Tongue-in-cheek, I quickly add that I'll take their money so that they value what they're getting. I also add that if I didn't take their money, they would not respect me. But the truth is I'd rather be talking to them or writing this book than anything else in the world. I love the experience of motivating and inspiring people through the spoken and the written word.

I also have the advantage of always thinking and talking about my passion: exciting people into success. I think more than I do. What do I mean? Well, I'll deliver three to four programs per week. Most my programs are 90 minutes to three hours long. That means I have a lot of "in-between-game" time to reinvent my content and stay fresh. I'm not so busy trying to make a living that I forget to make a life.

It took me thirty-five years to find something I truly love doing, and it's been worth it. Perhaps you're twenty and you're already immersed in your passion - you're one of the lucky ones. Or maybe you're forty and you haven't yet found yours. Keep looking. If you focus on your What, Why and How, you'll hit your Sweet Spot sooner than you think.

**LIVE IN THE
SWEET
SPOT.**

STEP 2: Expect More

See More.

Have More.

Be More.

Your "Expect More" Self-Exploration

Here is a simple 10 point test to determine your command of this skill. For each question, rate yourself on a scale of 1-10.

- [ ]   • I love change

- [ ]   • I'm always looking for new opportunities

- [ ]   • There is no doubt I will achieve my goals in the next year

- [ ]   • I have a turned-on personal vocabulary

- [ ]   • I always expect the best to happen in any situation

- [ ]   • I am outstanding at solving problems

- [ ]   • I bounce back quickly from setbacks

- [ ]   • I help others become more optimistic

- [ ]   • I will find a way or make a way to succeed in any situation

- [ ]   • I handle unexpected challenges well

◯ total

- **If you scored between 85 and 100**
Congratulations. You're already a Tough-Minded Optimist.
- **If you scored between 70 and 84**
You're already positive, you just need to kick it up a notch.
- **If you scored less than 70**
You need to turn around your attitude towards your future.
This chapter will help you get Juiced.

Expect: *to look forward to; regard as likely to happen; anticipate the occurrence or coming of; look out for; await; confidently believe that an event will occur.*

(Webster's Dictionary)

> **Risk more** *than others think is safe.*
> **Care more** *than others think is wise.*
> **Dream more** *than others think is practical.*
> **Expect more** *than others think is possible.*
> **Cadet Maxim, USMA, West Point, New York**

How are you feeling right now? Motivated? Just OK? Restless? Excited? Anxious? Tired? Depressed? Overwhelmed? Optimistic? In Control? Psyched and Hyped? Or Down and Out?

Your response is a direct function of what you expect to happen next.

Think for a moment about the following questions. Write down your answers. Do not proceed further until you've done this. Record the first thoughts that come to mind but don't rush them.

What do you expect to happen at work tomorrow? Next week? Next month? Next year?

What do you expect to happen at home tomorrow? Next week? Next month? Next year?

What do you expect of yourself tomorrow? Next week? Next Month? Next year?

What do you expect of other people tomorrow? Next week? Next month? Next year?

Here's what I expect:

At work: I expect to be challenged, stretched and tested. Tomorrow I will encounter a massive opportunity to grow my franchise. Next week, I will help two thousand people become more proactive and persuasive. Next month will be my best month ever. Next year, I will be recognized by the top 1000 companies in the United States and Canada as one of the ten best motivational speakers in North America.

At home: I expect love, loyalty and surprises. Tomorrow, our family will have a magical Friday night dinner together at a favourite restaurant. Next week, I'll bond closer with my wife even though I'm going on a road trip. Next month, my nineteen-year-old twins and my eleven-year-old daughter's development will fascinate me. Next year, this family will really come together as each member hits their sweet spot.

Of myself: I expect to grow, mature and prosper. I expect myself to stay enthusiastic and energized. I expect myself to be indestructibly optimistic. I expect myself to be a model to others. Tomorrow, I expect myself to thrill my clients. I expect myself to make my family feel safe and loved. Next week, I expect myself to perform at my Personal Best in every one of my seven motivational sessions. Next month, I expect myself to complete this book. Next year, I expect myself to give back more to the industry that has given me so much.

Of others: I expect people to consistently amaze me with their goodwill, integrity and warmth. Tomorrow, I expect my Clients to enjoy being with me and embrace my ideas. Next week, I expect my audiences to resonate with my message. Next month, I expect my partners and colleagues to perform like the world-class people and professionals they are. Next year, I expect at least 10 000 people to break through to their next level as a result of the messages in this book and my seminars.

It took me about an hour to write down my expectations of work, home, myself and others. How long did it take you? How are you feeling right now as a result of having written down your expectations? I'm grateful. I'm awed. I'm juiced. I'm amazed at what I've recorded.

By clearly defining my expectations, I've taken charge of what will happen next. Now, I'll back my expectations with the right actions.

I hope that, like me, you're bullish on the future. If you're not, the future is not going to be what you want it to be. **Pessimists attract problems. Optimists attract opportunities. Whatever you're looking for, that's what you'll find. If you expect more, you'll find more. Not** always. But the Law of Great Expectations always manifests itself over time: like attracts like. Positive results accrue to people with positive expectations.

Be a Neophile not a Neophobe. You'll live longer, perform better and have more fun.

A Neophile is someone who loves change while a Neophobe is someone who fears it. A Neophile feels the stress of change, but it's the good stress. It's what psychologists call "Eu-stress." This is the stress that ignites one's personal motivation to rise to fresh challenges. "Eu-stress" is the octane that drives outstanding performance.

A neophobe, on the other hand, experiences "dis-stress" when faced with change. This is the stress that retards personal performance. It can also lead to ill health and pain. According to the *Wall Street Journal* (12/26/03), scientists at the University of Chicago found that neophobia, fear of novelty, shortens lifespan – at least in rats. Neophobes were 60 per cent more likely to die at any time than their novelty-loving brothers.

As a motivator and social researcher, I can tell you that neophobia may not kill humans, but it certainly makes them miserable and myopic. Neophobes do not catch fire. In fact, they don't even see the fire when it's burning all around them. As the old Mexican proverb states, "No one can awaken a man who pretends to sleep."

Expect More, don't Hope for More.

One of the fundamental psychological discoveries of the past 100 years is that the human mind cannot tell the difference between that which you imagine and that which is really happening. Perception is reality. Nothing is anything but thinking that makes it so. So what are you imagining? What are the expectations you're setting for yourself that will make your reality a beautiful place to be?

Think about it: your expectations are the source of everything that follows. Unless they are fresh and healthy, how can anything else be?

What's more, you're in total control of your expectations. No one knows what the future will yield. Today's experts are tomorrow's idiots. Seriously, how many wise pundits do you know who got the future entirely wrong, not just once but repeatedly? So when someone shakes their head at you, look within. Protect your expectations and they'll protect you.

I'll share this story with you. When I first arrived in Canada in 2001, I merchandized myself to a number of speakers' bureaus — agents who promote speakers to companies and associations. Except for one, all of them told me that I would struggle to make a living as a professional speaker in Canada and the United States. Time and time again, they warned me that I was setting my expectations too high. The competition was too entrenched, they said. The clients were too cynical, they said; my "outsider status" was too much of a disadvantage, they said.

One agent, Martin Perelmuter, believed in me. Martin is the president of Speakers' Spotlight, Canada's leading professional speakers bureau. He stated that there was no limit to the success and the revenue we could generate together. His encouragement was all I needed. As I write this, I am officially Canada's top speaker as measured in engagements delivered per year. I don't tell you this to impress you. I say it to impress upon you that if you expect it, and you're willing to play full out, it will come to you.

Like any start-up, I worked my 70-hour weeks. I endured my sleepless nights. I withstood rejection after rejection without losing resolve. At least it was Canada where the rejections were oh-so-polite. Except they weren't rejections at all. They were just delayed approvals by people who temporarily couldn't appreciate quality.

I expected more and my expectations were all I had to hold on to. Then I was commissioned by a leading advertising agency, Ogilvy & Mather, to inspire their employees and clients. At the session were IBM, American Express, GlaxoSmithKline and Kraft Foods. All four companies hired me. Executives from those companies recommended me to other companies and the momentum keeps on growing.

My story isn't unique. It's the hallmark of Champions. It's called faith. It's called refusal-to-give-up. It's called test-driving-your-dream-in-advance. It's proof of the power of Expecting More.

Notice that the title of this chapter is "Expect More" not "Hope For More." What happens when you "hope" that something will happen? Do you feel totally certain that you'll get what you want? Or is there doubt? Say aloud right now, "I hope I achieve all my goals this year." Now say with conviction, "I expect to achieve all my goals this year."

What was the difference in how you felt? When you hope for something, it's merely a wish. Hoping may even increase your uncertainty because part of you also anticipates not getting what you want. So fear increases in lockstep with desire. Expecting, as per the superb *Webster's Dictionary* definition, is when you "regard as likely to happen; confidently believe that an event will occur."

Words are the labels you apply to your experiences. Nothing in life has any meaning except the meaning you give it. Develop a Juiced Personal Vocabulary.

At Environics/Lipkin, we've established a Personal Best Practice called "A Juiced Personal Vocabulary." We define it as follows:

Engaging in internal dialogue that honours and helps oneself; interpreting events in such a way that they keep one optimistic and motivated; practicing self-observation and vigilance to guard against a negative mindset; a unique "signature" personal vocabulary, packed with emotion and passion; understanding the role one plays in the life of others and being able to talk to them in the way they want to be spoken to.

Be quiet and listen to the next fifteen seconds without moving. What did you hear? The noises around you? The breathing of the person next to you? The growling of your stomach? The hum of your computer? The wind outside? Perhaps. But what did you hear inside your head? Hmm? The words that you were speaking to yourself – your thoughts.

You were thinking about why I was asking you to do this exercise. In fact, you were thinking four times faster than you talk. We speak at the rate of about 200 words a minute. But we speak mentally to ourselves at the rate of 800 words a minute. **What's more, our internal dialogue is incessant – every second of every hour of every day of every week of every month, awake or asleep. No wonder James Allen wrote: "As a man thinks, so he becomes."** Or as Descartes said: "I think, therefore I am."

Read the words below and, as you do so, think about how you feel:

*   Having an intense argument with someone
*   Losing your temper
*   Making a complete fool of yourself
*   A car accident
*   Failing your most important exam
*   Watching a husband and wife shout at each other
*   Having dinner at an exquisite restaurant with your favourite person
*   Winning $5 million in the national lottery
*   Enjoying a three-week Caribbean vacation
*   Closing your biggest deal
*   Kissing the person you love most
*   Climbing to the top of Mount Everest
*   Skydiving

What happened? Each set of words triggered a corresponding set of thoughts in your brain. And each set of thoughts triggered a corresponding set of emotions. And each set of emotions triggered a corresponding desire to take certain actions. So what are the thoughts that live inside your head? Do they trigger powerful and positive emotions most of the time? Are you consciously choosing your thoughts? Are they continually motivating you? Or are they holding you hostage? Are they the source of tension, worry and anxiety? Are you always expecting more? Or are you expecting less?

Be vigilant. From this moment on, engage in continual "Mind-Checks" every day or even every hour if necessary. For example, as I'm writing these words, I know that I have a deadline that's just a few weeks away. I also know that unless my partners like what I've written, you won't even be reading them. I could think about the possibility of failure and I could get worried and depressed.

Personally, however, my creativity dries up when I'm anxious. So I have to consciously think about the exhilarating rewards of success. I have to think and write as though it is impossible to fail. I have to saturate myself in the thoughts and emotions of success. In fact, I make myself experience all the ecstasy and fulfillment of success in advance. My expectations of the future become my current reality.

This is not complicated. It doesn't take the IQ of an Einstein to figure it out. What it does take is the tenacity and practice to follow it through - day in and day out. And, by the way, I'm not telling you to ignore the problems. As a good friend of mine advised me, "Trust in God, but lock up your camels."

Expect More. Two simple words that are easy to understand. What's tough is living the discipline of "Expecting More." What's tough is keeping the faith when the game momentarily turns against you. What's tough is describing your challenges in language that juices you to take yourself to the next level.

Whatever your problems, consciously see them in a light that empowers you – and this includes people problems. If you are angry with someone, you allow him to live rent-free in your mind. So whatever he may have done to you, think about him differently. Let it go or it's going to bring you down.

Dr. Martin Seligman, author of *Learned Optimism*, takes it a step further. He states that **the fundamental trait of people who sustain their levels of optimism in the face of adversity is their ability to interpret events to themselves in an empowering manner.** So, for example, if they were salespeople who had not made a sale to a prospect, they would not consider themselves to have been rejected. They would simply have benefited from a learning experience. Or they would have been through a dress rehearsal for the next attempt to sell to the prospect.

How do you explain adverse events to yourself? Do you consistently empower yourself? Or are you wearing away your resilience from within? There's always a positive meaning in any experience – you just have to find it. Recently, I was asked how I manage to consistently sustain my bullish outlook on life. "It's easy," I responded. "I attend all my own seminars." Seriously, you're not crazy if you talk to yourself as long as you say the right words.

Be self-aware.

Jim Balsillie, the CEO of Research-In-Motion (creators of the BlackBerry), told me that he looks for people who are "intensely self-aware." They must be aware of what's going on around them and inside of them. Their mental radar must be highly developed in order to move at the kind of speed that's mandatory for anyone who wants to thrive in the current environment. How aware are you of what's going on inside your cranium? Would you pass Balsillie's test? Without self-awareness, very little else happens.

Try this simple technique for enhancing self-awareness. I call it MCTV – Mental Circuit Television. Wherever you are, and whomever you are with, pretend that there is a video camera mounted on a surface just above your head. Imagine that this camera is filming you as you interact with the people around you. Then, imagine that this camera feeds into a screen in your skull. Watch yourself. Watch your thoughts. Watch your responses while they're happening. Listen to the words that you're using.

Ask yourself whether you're enhancing or decreasing both your well-being and the well-being of the people around you. Then reinforce or change your behaviour. Do whatever it takes. Don't be inhibited by your past behaviour or conditioning. Have the guts to do what you know you have to do, even if it feels awkward. And it will, until you do it often enough for it to become natural.

Let me ask you this question: what kind of words do you use to communicate with yourself, especially when you make a mistake? Do you insult yourself? Do you beat yourself up with phrases like:

You idiot! You fool! I can't believe you could be so stupid. Isn't that just typical? How could you be so dumb? You'll never be able to do it. You're out of the game. What a loser! You're hopeless. They'll never accept that. It'll never work. I'm at the end of my rope. It's just a matter of time before they find out I'm stupid. I'm just a fraud.

Just saying those words to yourself will drain you of all motivation and optimism. Instead, **the Champions have learnt to consciously talk to**

themselves in a way that sustains their spirit, especially in the tough moments. They're on a permanent mental diet. Whenever they're tempted to use abusive mental vocabulary, they replace it with words like:

You're only human. You gave it your best shot. Ten out of ten for hanging in there. It's just the first innings in a long life. What a great lesson! It's only a matter of time before you succeed. The most you can do is the most you can do. No one always bats a thousand. You're still in the game. I'm proud of you. You learned a lot today. It can only get better. Find a way or make a way. This is just a test. Now you really get to stretch yourself. You've got the right stuff, show it. I didn't fail; I just got results I didn't expect. Let's go again. Bring it on!

So, if you catch yourself insulting yourself, stop. I'm not saying that you should go soft on yourself. You and I need to hold ourselves to the highest internal standards. But above all else, we need to respect ourselves. The person who doesn't respect himself cannot respect anyone else. The person who abuses himself abuses others and gets abused by others in return. What goes on inside you determines what goes on around you. So begin building your own internal vocabulary of honour, respect and forgiveness.

Here's the neat thing about what I'm asking you to do: your everyday life becomes your laboratory for personal development. Every external event becomes an opportunity to experiment with an internal thought. Stay self-aware, especially in the pressure moments. Notice what works. Notice the results. Do more of what works.

Effective self-communication is just the beginning. If you want to be On-Fire, you have to love communicating with others.

It's our ability to communicate with others that is so vital to being On-Fire. A Juiced Personal Vocabulary is a rare skill. Think about how few people around you consistently use words that excite you. Think about how few people around you have the ability to generate empathy with others through their words and gestures. Now think how readily you respond to those who do.

If Expecting More is a way of expanding your view of what's possible, a Juiced Personal Vocabulary is how you get others to enrich their perspective. And once you widen their horizons, they can never go back to seeing the world the same way. A mind, once expanded, can never retreat to its original dimensions.

How well do you communicate with your stakeholders? What kind of words are you using to connect with them? Tomorrow morning, do a "verbal audit" of the words you use in the next 24 hours. Take inventory of both the positive and negative words that you consistently use with others. Take stock of how much time you spend complaining, gossiping or making excuses. If you're like sixty percent of the people I've observed and interviewed, you may discover that more than half of everything you say is negative in its orientation.

So how much do you enjoy communicating with others? What impact are your words having on the people around you? Do you even know? **Are you a one-person recession? Or are you a generator of success and possibility? Is your vocabulary bland? Or do you have a signature way of speaking that sets you apart from the crowd?**

If you don't enjoy the process of communication, you can never master a Juiced Personal Vocabulary. Not everyone can be a Churchill, Kennedy or Trudeau. But I promise you that everyone can increase their ability to move people simply by packing more enthusiasm, intensity and authenticity into their vocabulary. Nothing persuades people like genuine, unfiltered passion. So keep your negativity to yourself, but don't hold back the positive emotions. Let them flow. Loosen your stiff upper lip. Let down your guard. Blow away your buffer zone. If you have to go against the grain of your natural reserve, then do it.

Think about this: isn't communication really all about the transfer of emotions? Aren't words just packages of feelings? Yes, there may be times when you think you're just providing the facts. But even then, your communication will put the other person or people into some kind of emotional state. So develop your own brand of linguistic emotion - the kind that moves people to action.

If you're still unclear about what I'm saying here, listen to the way fans talk about their favourite sports. Listen to the impassioned reporting of the TV and radio sportscasters. Listen to the coaches and the players. What do you hear? Total engagement. Total commitment. Total animation. That's the way we should talk about every aspect of our lives. You'll be amazed at the response. I know. This is how I make a living. I focus on using words that are brimming with energy, vigor and possibility.

A Juiced Personal Vocabulary is the language of higher expectations. By using it, you become a carrier of promise and potential. Conviction is contagious. If you can help others Expect More, you'll start your own mini-movement. As the people around you get what they want, they'll help you get what you want. Given enough proof, even the cynical become converted. All it takes to start a fire is a spark. Be one.

"Expectations May Alter Outcomes Far More Than We Realize" (*The Wall Street Journal*, 11/07/03)

"Expectation becomes a self-fulfilling prophecy," says Robert Rosenthal, professor of psychology at the University of California, Riverside. "When teachers have been led to expect better intellectual performance from their students, they tend to get it. When coaches are led to expect better athletic performance from their athletes, they tend to get it. When behavioral researchers are led to expect a certain response from their research subjects, they tend to get it."

More alarming is how little known the expectation effect is. And that means there is a good possibility that some of the effects we attribute to a particular cause – from the benefits of smaller class sizes to the health-improvement effects of wealth – actually reflect the power of expectations.

So what's your Expectation Effect? Are your expectations of future performance bigger than your present? Or are they shrinking? Because if your expectations are growing smaller, so are you.

If Focus concentrates your energy on The Main Thing, Expecting More increases it. Expectations are magnifiers. If you confidently believe that an event will occur, you are far more likely to move towards it. When I stand in front of an audience, I expect with total certainty that I'll dazzle and delight them. My expectations are broadcast in my voice, signaled in my body language and reflected in my words. If they waiver, even for a moment, my hesitation becomes immediately apparent.

On the other hand, if you're highly doubtful that an event will occur, your ambivalence alone will endanger it. Negative expectations are the archenemy of personal achievement. They're the termites of the soul. Expectations become habitual. We develop a certain "Expectational Style." Fear of defeat replaces the will to win. Suspicion replaces trust. And timidity replaces boldness.

An Empowered-Expectational-Style requires a willingness to risk disappointment. The number one reason why people are afraid to expect more is that they're afraid of being hurt, disillusioned or embarrassed. Their anticipation of pain outweighs their anticipation of pleasure. To those people, I have three words: Get Over It.

Of course you're going to be disappointed. Of course, people are going to let you down. Of course, you're going to fall on your face. The future sucks sometimes. That's called life. And that's why an Empowered-Expectational-Style is so vital. It strengthens you against the gravitational pull of life's downfalls.

It's easy to become jaded. The clichéd admonishment I hear so often when I share my ambitious goals with others is "Be realistic." Translated: scale down your expectations; protect yourself against the pain of not getting what you want; play it safe; be reasonable; live between the lines.

My message? Be like Moses. Did he really part the Red Sea? Or was that simply a metaphor for the power of expectations. He expected to find a way to escape, both for himself and his people. His force of expectation created a powerful reality for himself and his followers. His pursuers didn't share his expectations and so they drowned – metaphorically speaking.

Here are some Expectation Enhancers that will help you expand your view of what's possible. These are questions designed to uncover the maximum potential of your present situation, irrespective of whether you interpret your current conditions as good or bad. What you regard as adversity can be your greatest gift. Life can only be lived forwards, but it can only be understood backwards. So ask yourself these questions, allowing yourself only positive, affirming responses:

Why am I designed to succeed where others have failed?
What makes me so powerful in this situation?
What can I do that no one else has done?
How can I get the people around me excited about this?
What makes my life so awesome?
How can I deliver spectacular service to my clients, colleagues, friends and family?
How can I act in such a way that others are inspired by my behaviour?
What's the best thing about my work?
How come I got to be so lucky to have such great friends, family, colleagues, clients?
What do I need to do to become the person I dream of being?
Who can I model who is already getting the results I want?
What is fabulous event is likely to happen in the next week, month and year?
How am I going to feel when I achieve my compelling outcomes?

Add your own questions. I want to see them. Send them to me:
mike.lipkin@environics.ca.

This book would never have been possible if it wasn't for the heightened Expectation Effect on myself. My business model calls for a book per year. I have to publish a new book every twelve months because the book comprises my speaking material. I get bored with my story long before anyone else. That's what keeps me fresh and relevant to my clients. There is nothing sadder than someone who keeps trying to drag out the same story year after year.

I chose the theme of Personal Consistency because it's so relevant to the challenges facing all of us. Then I simply expected to find the inspiration and the information to write the book in the six-month time frame I allocated myself. Yes, I had the discipline to follow through because my entire livelihood depended on it. But my expectations created the space, time and energy for the book to manifest itself.

So invest the time in setting your Raised Expectations. Make them SMART: Specific, Measurable, Actionable, Relevant and Time-related. Depending on your urgency, it may take you an hour, a day, a week, a month or a year. I know a high level executive who is taking a year sabbatical in Europe to decide what to do next. There are many things I'm asking you to do in the book, but this may be one of the most important. **Ultimately you don't get what you deserve; you don't get what you need; you get what you expect. So why not Expect More? You have no idea what you're capable of achieving.**

What's Your Past Win-Lose Record?

"What's past is prologue," wrote Shakespeare. "What brought you to this point will carry you to the next," says Lipkin. So what brought you to this point? Has your life-ride been rough or smooth? Have you had it easy? Or has it been hard? Were you born with a silver spoon in your mouth? Or have you had to eat crow?

Hey, I'm 46 years old. I've been to places I never want to visit again. I have a triple Ph.D. in failure, burnout and depression. I've been suckered. I've had dreams that turned into nightmares. I've had friends who turned into foes. I've had times when it took all I had just to keep up with the losers.

In other words, I have a history very similar to yours. But here's what keeps me juiced: Everything I've been through has happened for a single reason – to bring me to where I am right now. Wherever I am right now is where I'm supposed to be right now because that's where I am right now. And wherever you are right now is where you're supposed to be right now because that's where you are right now. You can't debate that fact. What you can debate is where you're going.

Think about the past year. Has it been a good one for you? Have you consistently achieved big goals that raised your expectations of yourself? Or has life been one disappointment after another? Have you dared greatly? Or have you stayed on the sidelines? Have people come through for you? Or have they let you down?

If your recent past has been positive, you're endowed with a huge advantage. You have a reservoir of empowering memories to dip into. The future can be a continuation of where you've been. You have momentum.

Confidence is largely a result of having done something successfully before. Someone who is used to winning expects to win more than someone who isn't. It's that simple. Winning becomes a state of mind that's expressed in every word and action.

Acting like you expect to get into the end zone is often the most effective way of getting there. It's far easier to achieve Personal Consistency when you're on a roll. As Joe Namath said, "When you're winning, nothing hurts." That's why I savour my wins so intensely. I want to ensure the taste, sound, sight, feel and smell of each win is registered at the deepest level of my psyche. I want the self-image of a champion embedded in my DNA.

I may be positive but I'm not Pollyanna. I know I'm going to lose a few. I know that not everyone likes my style. I know there will be times I'm off when I need to be on. I know things will go wrong, mistakes will be made and people will be mad at me. That's when I need my inventory of wins to sustain me.

This is my third book in four years. The first two have sold over 10 000 copies each exclusively through my seminars and website. I expect this book to sell over 10 000 copies like I expect the sun to rise tomorrow morning. My past experience is the biggest contributor to my Great Expectations. It never gets easier. But I get better.

On the other hand, if your recent past has been negative, your challenge is to leave it behind and grab onto something new. We'll explore this later in Chapter Six. The point here is to be aware of the impact of yesterday so it doesn't screw up tomorrow. The past doesn't equal the future unless you choose to live there.

Expecting More is even more important if you're trying to let go of your past. It requires even more of a conscious effort. Hold onto your Expectations. They're your lifeline to the future, especially when it seems like your past is always a step ahead of you. If you relentlessly Expect More, your fortune will turn. It always does – when you least expect it and when you're closest to giving up.

If there is a theme to my life, it's that my biggest wins always come after my biggest disappointments. It's called the Symmetry of Success.

How about you? Think about when you've hit the jackpot. Hasn't it been after a major setback? Wasn't your success a direct function of your setback? In fact, wasn't the setback merely preparation for the success? In other words, maybe there are no such things as failures or setbacks. Maybe there are just stages of ultimate successes.

It's called The Symmetry of Success. The *Oxford Dictionary* defines symmetry as, "*the beauty resulting from the correct proportion of the parts of a thing.*" Our so-called failures or setbacks are merely parts of the thing called Your Personal Best. Our challenge, therefore, is to ensure that we place all our experiences in the correct proportion for *our* lives. What's right for Mike Lipkin may be wrong for you. We all have different thresholds of tolerance. But one thing's for sure: a life without failures or setbacks is not a life at all. It's merely time spent in no-man's land – that twilight zone between pain and pleasure where numbness and caution replace true fulfillment and contentment.

I don't know what's right for you, but here's a core belief of the hundreds of extraordinary achievers with whom I've had the privilege of working over the past five years: **disappointments are just tests of character, tenacity and faith.** They are the gateway to the next level. They only mean that we didn't achieve our desired result when we wanted to achieve it. If you choose to become angry and frustrated over your disappointments, you are simply condemning yourself to a cycle of even deeper disappointment. On the other hand, if you embrace your disappointment as a gift, you'll discover both the strategy and the timing to achieve your objectives. And, just as important, you'll acquire the emotional equilibrium to sustain your success.

So try this crazy idea the next time you're disappointed: wherever you are, stand up and shout (even if it's only to yourself), "YES! I LOVE THIS DISAPPOINTMENT. I'M ABOUT TO BREAK THROUGH TO THE NEXT LEVEL." Your colleagues will probably think you're nuts but you know what? They'll probably smile; they may even laugh; they'll certainly require an explanation for your eccentric behaviour and they'll probably end up putting the "disappointment" in the right perspective as well.

If you Expect More, you become an Adaptive Navigator.

"Can You See It?" asks the tagline in IBM's advertising. Can you see what, exactly? What other people don't see. The opportunities, the trends; the changes; the patterns; the pitfalls; the subtleties visible only to the Expectationally Gifted.

Of all the talents that will make you successful in the 2000s, seeing those things that others cannot see may be the most vital. With everything on fast-forward, life becomes a blur. The urgent need to get things done becomes a blinker that blocks our view. For the vast majority of people, just surviving a world gone crazy is a big enough aspiration.

Here's an extraordinary statistic: the Environics' Social Values Research has found that only 22 per cent of Canadians express an attraction to risk and complexity. 40 per cent of people express an active aversion to it. 38 per cent are caught in no-man's land, not quite sure how they feel about it.

That means that only **22 per cent of people expect themselves to thrive on risk and complexity. They look for the opportunities offered up by risk and complexity. They apply a powerful Personal Best Practice called Adaptive Navigation.**

Environics/Lipkin defines *Adaptive Navigation* as: *having the flexibility and mental openness to adapt to unforeseen events that interfere with the realization of one's goals; discovering, developing and implementing alternative strategies to achieve one's goals; unbreakable belief in one's own ability to solve any problem; personal conviction that there are always favourable options in any situation; enthusiasm for technology as a powerful tool for responding to the demands of everyday life; use of strong personal purpose as a compass to guide oneself through massive change; perpetual fascination with life and all its challenges.*

Adaptive Navigators understand the rhythm and tempo of change. They don't seek to hold onto what's gone, they don't seek to control the uncontrollable, and they don't seek to know the unknowable. Instead, they plug themselves into the Zeitgeist of change. Zeitgeist comes from the German words "Zeit" which means "time" and "Geist" which means "spirit."

Think about it: if you were totally immersed in the "spirit of the time you're living in," wouldn't you be truly effective? Are you? You don't have to know the millions of minutiae that are changing every nanosecond. Instead, you need to see the patterns that are emerging as they change.

The difference between Adaptive Navigators and Struggling Stragglers is often just the filter through which they process their everyday experiences and information. Adaptive Navigators look for the meaning behind the obvious; they're continually alert to the consequences of what's going on around them; they're constantly making a movie of the future, scene by scene, theme by theme; there's no such thing as a "good" or "bad" development, there's just "significant" or "insignificant."

They maximize their exposure to the Zeitgeist through consumption of media, the Internet and, most importantly, speaking to as many people as possible. There is no substitute for live human interaction. No survey, article, broadcast or website can replace the emotional or intellectual value of meaningful dialogue. No matter how wired you may be, you cannot be Howard Hughes and expect to be an Adaptive Navigator.

So whether you're shy or whether you're PT Barnum, you have to be gregarious. You have to develop a fascination with other people – especially if they're different from you, and especially if you believe they're in tune with the times. That's how you develop the acute personal radar that sees opportunities where others see nothing.

INC. MAGAZINE (November 2003) calls the individuals who are ahead of the curve "The Prophetic Minority." These are the "canaries in the cage of the consumer culture." They are the individuals who ignite the trends that sweep the rest of us along with them. If you're lucky and connected enough, you can engage them personally. Otherwise, they can be followed on the Internet by visiting sites in categories such as "Consumer Advocacy and Information" or "Consumer Opinion" or "Social Trends" or "Thought Leaders" or "News Makers."

You can also engage The Prophetic Minority in your own company or community. I've identified ten people in my immediate business circle who are plugged into the Zeitgeist. Sometimes I call them to find out what's new. Other times, I call them to reinforce or disprove my own opinions. I can tell you that I would feel adrift without them. They're my extra set of eyes, ears, gut and nose. Just knowing that they're there reinforces my confidence and sense of well-being. Make sure you find yours.

Adaptive Navigation is where experience, curiosity and naiveté intersect to produce inspired judgment. There is no room for cynicism.

As soon as you're finished reading the next paragraph, go and look into the eyes of any Adaptive Navigator nearby. Irrespective of his or her age, you'll see the incandescent glow of perpetual wonder. They are perennially fresh. They love their odyssey through life and it shows. They expect life to show them where to go. And it does.

Just a few minutes in an Adaptive Navigator's company will energize you. You know why? Because your faith in the promises of life will be restored. Adaptive Navigators are living proof that anything is possible. To quote Timex, "They take a licking and they keep on ticking." In fact, they keep on getting better, one day at a time, year after year.

Consciously or unconsciously, Adaptive Navigators know that they have all they'll ever need to thrive at any given moment. They are always option-rich, that's why they're well beings. Adaptive Navigators always know how to do it, how to learn how to do it, or how to find someone to help them do it. But they are not delusional. If they're trained as marketers or salespeople, they're not going to volunteer for an assignment in civil engineering. They play off their strengths.

Our most stressful moments are when we believe that we have no options. That's when we become desperate. That's when we hear people say: "It's hopeless" or "I've tried everything" or "It's impossible." Well, the instant you believe that you have no options, you lose all your personal power. Desperation and panic are intertwined. They cloud our judgment and literally make us sick. Think about it: desperation and panic are not just emotions; they are physical states that make us do things that we *always* regret later on. Worry, fear and anxiety *can* kill you emotionally, financially and ultimately physically.

Adaptive Navigators don't waste time or energy lamenting what should be or what might have been. The way life is, is the way life should be, because that's the way life is. They know that delays are not denials. So they deal with them. They know that they'll ultimately triumph. They don't groan; they grow. They have a sense of certainty that a risk taken will reward the risk taker – even if the final outcome is not entirely clear at the outset.

Dr. David Jamieson, head of the Environics Advanced Analytics Unit, believes that Adaptive Navigators have something that their less aware counterparts do not – Vigilance to Opportunity. They engage in "implicational thought." By that he means they look for the implications of the immediate events and circumstances around them. Some people are naturally gifted in intuiting implications and opportunities. But it is a skill that can be learnt. It begins with asking the critical question, "What does this mean?" It entails talking to as many people as possible, staying open, scanning the media and being genuinely curious about one's environment.

Here's a neat assignment for you: in the next week, commit yourself to exploring the implications of one significant event around you. Take it all the way: use Google to do the research, talk to people who are experts on the subject, get curious, ask great questions. And let me know what you've found.

Make this exercise a habit. **Curiosity never killed the cat. It gave the cat its many lives so it could out-live, out-eat and out-breed its competition.** Look beyond the obvious and you'll see exactly what you need to see. As my partner, Michael Adams, instructs, "Torture the data until it tells the truth."

Importantly, Adaptive Navigators may not always have been so adaptive; they have painstakingly built their unique bundle of skills and beliefs to succeed. What didn't kill them made them stronger. And perhaps their most important skill of all is simply "Problem Solving" – the ability to resolve difficult or complex matters quickly and effectively.

That's why your answer to the following question will determine whether you are literally worth a million dollars to your team or organization: *are you the go-to person when it comes to solving difficult problems?* If you answered "yes," I'd like to hear from you. Seriously, I want to meet you. The more Potent Problem Solvers I know, the greater my powers of Adaptive Navigation will be. Please e-mail me at mike.lipkin@environics.ca.

You see what you expect to see but it helps if you know how to look.

Here is the Adaptive Navigation Blueprint for Potent Problem Solving – eight steps to getting to the heart of any problem and finding a solution. It comprises the combined wisdom of some of the best problem solvers in the world. Use it, enjoy it, refine it and share it with others:

1. Know that you have the answers in advance. They just haven't been revealed to you yet. Continually expect that you're about to have a breakthrough. (*Truly believing that you have the answer in advance will program your subconscious to assist you.*)

2. Consciously love the problem. Be grateful for it. It's about to take you to the next level. (*Problems are like workout sessions for the brain. You need them to stay strong and supple.*)

3. Clearly define the problem, so that you and your stakeholders can genuinely understand not just the problem, but all the satellite issues around the problem. (*In many cases, a problem well defined is a problem solved.*)

4. Express your desired outcome in a way that motivates both you and your stakeholders. (*Know what you want and make sure that it really excites you and your stakeholders. Desire accelerates delivery.*)

5. Identify at least three ways of solving the problem – no matter how outlandish they are. If there are more, go for it. Don't get frustrated; stay fascinated. A lateral arabesque is often better than a frontal assault. (*The more options you have, the more well-being and sense of abundance you'll experience.*)

6. Evaluate the upside and downside of every option based on your desired outcome. Use your intuition, experience and available information to make a firm decision. (*At the start of the process, commit to making a decision by a certain time and then commit irrevocably to the decision. This alone can guarantee you success.*)

7. Execute the decision with fierce conviction. (*Once the decision is made, invest yourself fully in implementing it. Anything less will condemn you to failure.*)

8. Assess the astuteness of the decision and then constantly course-correct as you go along. Do not become emotionally attached to the decision. (*It's not the actual decision that determines your ultimate success, it's the spur to action followed by relentless adaptation.*)

Adaptive Navigation is first and foremost a team sport.

Complexity and Massive Change are not games for solo artists. I seek out kindred spirits who amplify my power. Adaptive Navigators attract other Adaptive Navigators. As members of similar tribes, they have an affinity for each other. And the more Adaptive Navigators you surround yourself with, the more powerful you become.

"Powerful people like to work and play with other powerful people," says Paul Bernard, an executive consultant who works with corporate and Wall Street clients. Indeed, they may not even make much distinction between business and pleasure, he said. "It's all about networking." (*New York Times*, 2/29/04)

That's why I chose Environics as my team when I came to Canada in 1999. In my native South Africa, I was a celebrated author, speaker and communication coach to the country's most successful companies. In Canada, I was a complete unknown in a very different climate with very different inhabitants. There was no way I could have achieved anything on my own.

My first contact with Environics was a direct result of Expecting More. Throughout 1999, I scanned the local Toronto newspapers and magazines for ideas and people who could become my team-members. Based on a decade of Expecting More, I knew it was only a matter of time before I found the resources I was searching for.

I read an article in the *Globe and Mail* by Michael Adams, President of the Environics Research Group, on the schizophrenic state of the Canadian psyche in December 1999. "If times are so good," the headline read, "Why do we feel so bad?" It went on to describe some of the key social trends transforming the U.S. and Canada. As I read the words, I knew I had found my future partner. I also knew instantly how I would pitch my promise to him.

I contacted Michael Adams. We met. I told him I liked the article. I also said I thought he used a lot of big words that many ordinary Canadians may not be able to understand. I told him that my specialty was making complex things simple. I pitched my vision to him: "I will help democratize the Environics Social Values Research so we can help the vast majority of Canadians make sense of things that don't make sense." I also promised him that we'd make a profit while we popularized his insights.

There was an immediate "simpatico" and eight months later we started up a joint venture called Environics/Lipkin. In the four years since then, I've spoken to over a million people in the U.S. and Canada, and sold over 40 000 books and CDs. We're also partnering with other Adaptive Navigators to change the world, one person at a time.

Environics/Lipkin has created The Personal Best Practices that I'm sharing with you throughout the book. Thousands of people are applying them to take themselves to a whole new level. If you want to know more about them, visit my website — www.mikelipkin.com. I've downloaded my entire book, *Your Personal Best*, on the site. You can also take the "Self-Explorations" on each Personal Best Practice and massively enhance your personal power.

By the way, you're welcome to do whatever you want with this information as long as you acknowledge where you got it. My definition of copyright is you have the right to copy. I make you this offer not because I'm a Good Samaritan. On the contrary, I'm a committed Capitalist who believes in altruism at a profit. I make you this offer because it's part of my strategy of Building Buzz.

I know you're a thought leader in your company or your community (like all the people who read my books). You're vocal and outgoing. People seek out your opinion. If you share my work with them, I profit from your credibility. You profit from my insights. The people who seek your counsel profit from our combined guidance. Expectations are raised. Everyone wins. It's a beautiful thing.

'Survivor' Meets Millionaire and a Show Is Born
(*The New York Times* 10/19/03)

If there's a Poster Boy for Expecting More, it's Mark Burnett, the executive producer of *Survivor, The Restaurant* and *The Apprentice*. As the *New York Times* reported:

> If there's one thing Mark Burnett has learned in his decade in television, it is this: never let an opportunity slip away.
>
> He put that opportunity to work when he found himself shooting the *Survivor* finale at the Wollman rink in Manhattan. Donald Trump, who happens to own the place, was there for the event. Though they had never met, Mr. Burnett walked right up and introduced himself.
>
> Two weeks after their initial encounter, Mr. Burnett called Mr. Trump and pitched *The Apprentice*, a reality TV show set in the business world. Mr. Trump said that when he was considering whether to do the show, he was swayed by the educa-

tional factor, and by the idea that it would be as brutal and real as any business transaction. Applicants came out in droves: 215 000 people in 13 cities auditioned for 16 slots.

Mr. Trump says of Mr. Burnett, "I don't think I've ever met anybody with a greater sense of curiosity." Mr. Burnett says he is thrilled to working so closely with his idol. "I'd like to have a go at his level," he admits. "I don't know if I'll ever make it. But you know something, if you're not shooting for the stars, you're not shooting."

"The Apprentice" became the highest rated TV show of the season. Burnett shot for the stars and hit them. Making iconic reality TV shows is his shtick. What's yours?

Expecting More also means Expecting The Unexpected

I can tell you this with total certainty: **the unexpected results of every action will always outnumber the expected results. Surprises should never take you by surprise. In fact, life is just one big surprise after another.**

When Jeffrey Immelt assumed the CEO position at General Electric in 2001, he said that in his first twelve months on the job he didn't have a single normal day. So what else is new? At Environics/Lipkin, we believe that Normal doesn't live any more and she's never coming back. She's been replaced by massive, continuous unpredictability. Disruption is the new daily routine.

Lipkin's 60-Day Law states that every two months, either your personal life or your professional world will be rocked by a major upheaval. If it's not, you're either playing it too safe or you don't know what's going on. In between, your weekly life will be impacted by a series of smaller, but no less intense convulsions.

Your "Surprise Readiness" will determine how well you perform in the "Personal Quake Zone" when so much depends on your immediate response. Think of your last Personal Quake. How effective were you? Are you proud of your behaviour? Was it your "finest hour"? Or do you cringe at the memory of how you behaved?

That's the true meaning of a Hero: someone who performs the way we would have liked to perform in the Quake Zone; someone who unleashed their Personal Best in the most adverse circumstances; someone who expected the most of herself and delivered against her own expectations.

That's the thought that I carry with me in adversity: how can I perform in such a way that I'll be proud of myself after the moment has passed? Like you, I encounter the unexpected daily. As someone who continually operates with one foot in the unknown, I'm always tripping. I'll never get used to the feeling of falling. I'll never enjoy the impact of mistakes on my psyche and self-esteem. It always hurts. But I expect to fall. And I expect to get up immediately. To quote an ancient Japanese proverb: fall down seven times, stand up eight.

It's especially tough to continue expecting more from others when those you trust betray you. It's happened to all of us. Disloyalty is nothing new. From Judas to Brutus and beyond, betrayals have been an occupational hazard, especially when the stakes are high and egos are big. Sometimes the betrayals are real, and sometimes they're imagined.

The challenge is to sustain your trust-ability in the face of perceived temporary treachery. Do not succumb to the siren cry of the Expect-Lessers: "That will teach me to trust people. I'll never trust anyone again." Better to be cheated once or twice than live your entire life in suspicion. So get over it when it happens. And get on with expediting your expectations.

Resilience:
1. The power or ability to return to the original form or position after being bent, compressed or stretched; elasticity;
2. Ability to recover readily from illness, depression, adversity or the like; buoyancy. (*Webster's Dictionary*)

Your expectations determine your resiliency. If you expect to bounce back from adversity, you will. If you expect to retain your elasticity, you will. If you expect to emerge from every situation faster, smarter, stronger, you will. I can tell you this because of all the resilient people I've researched over the past ten years.

The golden thread running through all their psyches was a conviction they would prevail. They defended themselves against denial. They embraced "what is." Saw "what could be." And they did "what could be done."

Doubt is the great enemy. Doubt destroys. It's the opposite of Expecting More. It's the mental assassin that slips past your defenses to kill your certainty. So stand guard at the door of your mind. Recognize doubt when it approaches. Protect yourself by Expecting More, even when everyone around you is expecting less.

Here's an AHA: the greatest opportunities present themselves to you when everyone is expecting less. Why? Because if people expect less, they do less. Less people pursue the Big Prize. Competition drops. Your premium rises. And your achievements garner even greater kudos. I see it all the time. Just Expecting More is enough to set you apart from the crowd. As long as you take action.

Zero Trauma

In the September 2003 issue of the *Harvard Business Review*, Gary Hamel and Liisa Valikangas describe provide an inspiring account of how to achieve resilience on both an individual and corporate level:

> The quest for resilience can't start with an inventory of best practices. Today's best practices are manifestly inadequate. Instead, it must begin with an aspiration: zero trauma. The goal is a strategy that is forever morphing, forever conforming itself to emerging opportunities and incipient trends. The goal is an organization (person) that is constantly making its future rather than defending its past. The goal is a company where revolutionary change happens in lightning-quick, evolutionary steps - with no calamitous surprises, no convulsive reorganizations, no colossal write-offs, and no indiscriminate, across-the-board layoffs. In a truly resilient organization (person), there is plenty of excitement but no trauma.

Raise your expectations to this level. Commit to achieving them. A high level of performance will follow.

I want to close this chapter by asking you to stay open.

"How do trend spotters find what they're looking for?" asks the *Wall Street Journal* (02/09/04). Answer: "They keep their eyes open." Talk to the experts on how they spot trends, and you're likely to get as many answers as there are experts. What they look for, whom they talk to, what they read - there are no easy answers. Some rely on obscure journals; others on key groups of people they think are ahead of the curve. Some pore over data; others follow the money. But if there's one common denominator, it's this: the best way to find out what's around the corner is to keep your mind – and your eyes – open.

Arnold Aronson, former CEO of Saks Fifth Avenue and now a top retailing consultant at Kurt Salmon Associates in New York, states that, "It's important at the top levels of an organization to spend time looking for big new ideas. Farther down, people aren't going to have as much time to break away from the daily demands of their job to do this. But good leaders should help set a culture where this intuition about what's next is rewarded."

How much time are you spending looking for the next new, new thing? How much time are you spending on helping those around you to do the same? How effectively are you communicating your expectations to others? How receptive are you to novel ideas and concepts that may fly in the face of your established paradigms?

Environics' Social Values Research shows a strong correlation between those individuals who have adapted marvelously to the new global complexity and a personal view that other people and other cultures have a great deal to offer. These new winners have an inclination to incorporate new influences into their own lives. They experiment. They continually create new mental models by fusing existing paradigms with new ideas and possibilities.

Expect to learn from the people around you and the people around you will become your teachers. What's more, **other people instinctively know when you're open to their point of view. You don't have to say a word for them to know whether you're receptive to their ideas. It's in the smile on your face, the tilt of your head, the curiosity in your eyes.**

A mind is like a parachute. It works best when it's open. It also evokes the law of reciprocal openness with others. I vocally honour the ideas offered to me by colleagues and clients not just because it's a Personal Best Practice, but also because my mental filter in every conversation is: what happens if this person is right? That question alone helps me extract the most empowering meaning from every conversation. My perspective is enriched and the other person wants to give me even more. If you want to be interesting to others, be interested in others.

LIVE IN THE
SWEET
SPOT.

STEP 3:
Be You

Be Authentic.
Be Courageous.
Be Idealistic.

3

Your "Be You" Self-Exploration

Here is a simple 10 point test to determine your command of this skill. For each question, rate yourself on a scale of 1-10.

- [ ] • I believe I'm a Powerful Person
- [ ] • I know exactly what I want others to think of me
- [ ] • I am good at building a high profile for myself
- [ ] • I am not afraid to be myself when I'm with colleagues and customers
- [ ] • I am willing to make lots of mistakes in pursuit of my goals
- [ ] • I am not afraid to look stupid in the eyes of others
- [ ] • I am an idealist
- [ ] • I have the courage to go against the crowd when I believe I have to
- [ ] • I'm willing to be vulnerable
- [ ] • I make it easy for others to be themselves when they're around me

◯ **total**

- **If you scored between 85 and 100**
Congratulations. You're already "Being You."
- **If you scored between 70 and 84**
You're "Almost You", you just need a little more confidence and courage.
- **If you scored less than 70**
You're trying to be what you're not.
This chapter will help you be authentic.

"I come from a long line of chiefs, stretching all the way back to Hawiiki where our ancient ones are...the ones that first heard the land crying and sent a man. His name was also Paikea, and I am his most recent descendent."

Paikea Apirana, *The Whale Rider*

Authentic: *1. not false or copied; genuine; real; original; primary. 2. reliable; trustworthy. 3. in harmony with the truth.* (Webster's Dictionary)

"Be You," the sign outside the old church declared, "because others are already taken."

That timely piece of advice has become my personal mantra. It's how I make a living. It's what I sell. It's what I do.

You're reading these words because you resonate with both the tone and the content of what I'm saying. You like my style. Something about my message and me connects with you. Maybe it's my energy, or maybe it's my sense of humour, or maybe it's the different perspective I'm helping you develop. The bottom line is that you like what Mike Lipkin stands for.

What do you stand for? What's your personal style? How would you describe the person you are? Why would I want to be around you? What about You makes you like yourself? What's your UPD – Unique and Powerful Difference? How are you morphing into the Most You that you can be?

After a decade of studying thousands of people who consistently perform at their Personal Best, I can offer you this truth: **People-On-Fire are totally invested in their own power.** What do I mean? They don't second-guess themselves. They have no doubt about their own ability. They radiate an aura of certainty that others find irresistible.

They have a personal charisma that comes from their commitment to being themselves. Sometimes the commitment is conscious (as in my case) and sometimes it's instinctive.

They don't burn away precious psychic energy trying to be what they're not. They're not trying to impersonate others in an attempt to be accepted by others.

They like who they are and what they stand for. They honour themselves, therefore they honour others. They celebrate their own lineage of chiefs in every act. They believe they're a gift to the people around them. And they inevitably are. They're authentic. Their integrity shines through. They're true to themselves. They're compelled to do the right thing even when it's the hardest thing. They don't flip flop on their beliefs or the actions they know they must take. Self-betrayal is not an option, therefore betraying others isn't either.

People-On-Fire keep getting better: their total investment in their own power motivates them to exercise their power more often than those who haven't made the investment. The more they do, the more powerful they become. The more they discover about their hidden treasure, the richer they become. And the virtuous cycle continues.

So that's what this chapter is all about — how to help you maximize the impact of your resources by being Fully-You.

In my seminars, I ask three simple Personal Branding Questions that most delegates cannot effectively answer, mainly because they've never truly thought about them. People spend their lives looking in the wrong direction. They keep looking for solutions outside of themselves when the real solutions always reside within.

And by the way, this is not New Age mumbo jumbo. This is core to achieving the Personal Consistency that is the difference between having it all and having it all disappear. Either you understand how to integrate the pieces of You into a growing personal powerhouse, or you'll disintegrate into a struggling survivor, barely making it through each brutal day.

Look around you. Look at how many people are hurting. Look at how few people relish the cataclysmic change around them. We're back to the "One Percenters."

Recently, I delivered a seminar to a group of pharmaceutical salespeople. There was a man in my audience called "Chuck." I asked Chuck what kind of people he enjoyed being with. "People who accept me for who I am," Chuck replied. "And who are you?" I asked. "I don't know," Chuck responded with a shrug.

So think about the Personal Branding Questions below. Write down your responses. Do not proceed further until you've completed this exercise:

   1. Who are you really? At the deepest level, what kind of person are you? How

would you describe yourself in 200 words or less? What's most important to you when it comes to life, relationships, and work? What makes you happy?

2. What are the values you wish to broadcast to the world? What do you want to represent to the people around you? Why are you "simply irresistible" to others (not just attractive, but irresistible)?

3. How are you ensuring personal memorability? What are your high-impact "Personal Brand Attributes" that differentiate you from the crowd?

I'll give you my responses to the above three questions and I want you to e-mail me yours – mike.lipkin@environics.ca.

I am the most enthusiastic person I know. I live to learn and grow. I'm turned on by doing things that no one has ever done before. I'm in constant search of the next break-through. I always feel as though I'm on the cusp of a breakout. I'm all about unleash-ing the energy in the people around me so they can also live in the self-actualization zone. I get a vicarious thrill when others live their dream. I love partnering with out-standing people to achieve results in the face of fierce competition. I will be worthy of my gifts by always playing full out. Life is a feast but I bring my own food for others.

When it comes to life, being recognized as extraordinary is vital to me. I have to inspire and empower others in order to be inspired and empowered. I have to constantly feel the rush that comes from igniting the "AHA" in other people's minds that motivates them to do what they were previously afraid to do. Feeling fully-engaged is central to my overall feeling of well-being.

When it comes to relationships, total openness and trust are fundamental. I never want to feel that anything is being hidden from me. I want people around me who will chal-lenge and stretch me. I want to feel how much they enjoy my presence. At the same time, I want them to give me frank, everyday feedback. I don't want subtlety when it comes to letting me know what I need to change. I want people around me who are at their best in wild times. I want people who share my fascination and joie de vivre.

When it comes to work, it must feel like play. I make no distinction between the two. I'm always doing both. What's important to me is that I must feel "positive fear" – the fear that comes from doing things that I'm not sure how to do, things that I've never done before. I must never feel bored or stagnant. I must be playing to my Picasso, my Unique-Talent that is my portal to personal greatness. I need to create buzz and I need to be surrounded by buzz.

What makes me happy is when I'm in a state of flow, when the best of me comes out of me effortlessly. Sometimes it happens when I'm on stage and sometimes it happens when I'm helping Dani-Emma, my eleven-year-old daughter, with her homework. Sometimes, it happens at the gym as I head into the fiftieth minute of intense cardio-vascular exercise. Sometimes, like now, it's when the words manifest themselves magically on a screen in front of me. Sometimes, it's in a look that I give someone on the subway and sometimes it's in a look that I receive. It's a feeling of weightlessness, of wonder, of absolute well-being.

I know this is what makes me happy so I seek it out any time, any place, with any one. And because that's what I'm seeking, that's what I find many times a day, every day.

Here are the values I wish to broadcast to the world (this book being one of my primary channels):

1. I want to represent energy, enthusiasm and excitement. I want to be a keeper of the flame. I want to light up others with my passion.

2. I want to represent a person at the edge of change. I want to be the surfer who catches the wave just before it breaks.

3. I want to represent a hybrid of knowledge and action. I want people to see me as a source of personal growth. I want to be the bridge between what people are and what they want to be.

4. I want to represent lightness, fun and enjoyment. I want to be a smile, the sound of laughter, a shout of triumph.

5. I want to represent everyday opportunity. I want people to see me and anticipate good things about to happen everywhere.

Here are my high-impact "Personal Brand Attributes" that differentiate me from the crowd:

- My association with Environics – one of Canada's most respected research houses.
- My international profile as an economic nomad who has worked in 28 countries with over a million people.
- My physical vitality, animation and extrovert style.
- My range of innovative programs.
- The bright and bold optics around my programs and promotional material.
- My alliances with outstanding people and thought leaders who help me build buzz.
- The advertising that I run in national media.

What are you doing? What could you do? And how does it mesh with the "Triumphant Triad" that we explored in the chapter on Focus?

There's no easy path to a Powerful Personal Brand. The quickest path is usually trial and error. But if you simply direct your energy towards the Three Personal Branding Questions, the way forward will eventually present itself to you.

If there is a world-champion Personal Brand, it's Oprah Winfrey. Her fortune is estimated at $800 million and *Entertainment Weekly* has ranked her as the most powerful person in entertainment, ahead of Stephen Spielberg and Rupert Murdoch. Following the September 11 attacks, it was Oprah who led America's national memorial service.

According to the *National Post* (12/20/03), here's why Oprah has become the preeminent Personal Brand of our time: "Oprah, more than any of her imitators, has tapped into our cultural ideal of self-help by making it central to her public biography. Her struggles with her weight, her self-esteem and her childhood are offered as therapeutic triumphs over personal adversity. If suffering is the problem, for Oprah, self-transformation is the solution."

While Oprah may have more highly developed charisma glands than the rest of us mere mortals, she very clearly applies the three core principles of building a great Personal Brand:

1. She stands for something very specific – self-transformation.
2. She consistently broadcasts her authentic values to the world.
3. She seizes every opportunity to enhance the impact of her brand in a memorable way – from TV shows, to magazines to book clubs to movies.

I'm now going to ask you to do something that you may find very challenging, especially if you're Canadian: let other people know how good you are. This is not bragging or boasting. It's Personal Marketing. It's letting other people know in the most appropriate way the calibre of the contribution you're making to their success.

According to the *New York Times* (09/28/03), executive women, regardless of occupation or seniority, are often quite poor at self-promotion – and are hurt in their professional advancement as a result. Peggy Klaus, a communication coach, states, "A lot of professionals are having to compete as never before. How do you make yourself stand out? You have to control your own career, which means telling people what you're doing, what you've done and what you want." The people around you need you to help them understand your value to them. They're usually so busy trying to manage their own lives that they're not paying that much attention to the role that you're playing. So design your own marketing program. Maybe it's just a conversation or an e-mail letting them know what you've done. Or maybe it's a regular update of how you're helping them become successful.

My agent, Martin Perelmuter, has an endearing way of marketing his contribution to me: he always refers to "we" not "I." It's never "I got you another gig." It's always, "We've just got another gig". I know what he's doing for me but every time he tells me, I'm enthused because "we're" achieving the results together. Work out your Unique-Way.

Just as the sun always rises in the east, Your Personal Best is a direct function of your Embrace of Authenticity.

Think about this: when are you at your absolute best? When are you most charismatic? When do other people really love being around you? Isn't it when you're being authentic? Isn't it when you're totally natural and open? Isn't it when you're in a state of flow, relaxed and unselfconscious?

Here's the unchallengeable truth: We're all at our most wonderful when we reveal our authentic selves to the world. We're at our most powerful when we get rid of the mask and let our true energy show through. You know why? Because then ALL of our energy is invested in the moment. There's no wasted energy being burnt away by fear or hesitation. Our personal power is at its purest.

On the other hand, think about some of your most painful moments. Aren't they when you're forced to act in a way that goes against the grain of your character? Aren't they when you're forced to observe hollow rituals that have no meaning for you? Isn't it when you play the role that others expect you to play even while you feel uncomfortable or awkward playing it? So why do we do it? Well, sometimes, we may genuinely have no choice.

For many people, not being authentic is the norm. Worse still, many people are afraid to be authentic. They're afraid that they may reveal something of themselves to others that could be held against them later. Here's the core message of this chapter: **the original is always more valuable than the copy! The downside of being you is nothing, absolutely nothing, compared to the authentic power of being you.**

Your authentic actions are most often The-Real-You-In-Motion. I know that when I'm authentic in a positive way, I'm truly outstanding. I access wisdom and wit that I did not know I possessed. Somehow, it rises to the surface like a bubbling spring. As a professional speaker, I HAVE to be authentic. I can only rehearse so much – then I have to rely on the power of Authenticity to carry me through. In fact, I rehearse being authentic in advance. This is a technique where thorough preparation is combined with visualization and relaxation. I actually see myself being authentic with the audience and then I relax because I know that I know my subject.

The dark side of Authenticity is how we behave in our negative moments. Here's where we have to practice vigilance. Here's where we need to draw a line in our psyches between our good and bad emotions. With respect to our bad emotions, we need to control our authenticity; we need to rein it in tightly. So refuse to succumb to the rage. Instead of venting your distress on the people around you, use humour to defuse your temper. When your computer crashes or you get caught in the voicemail maze, recognise your micro-stresses for what they are – the potholes and pitfalls of 21st century everyday life.

Let me ask you this question: have you ever really lost your temper about something and then, afterwards, wondered how you could have ever got so angry? On the other hand, have you ever said to someone: "Don't worry, you'll laugh about this tomorrow"? Well, why wait? Laugh about it now.

People almost never do things just to annoy you. Whatever action they've taken, they took because they thought that was the right thing to do at the time.

And remember Robert Fulghum's immortal words: "Never confuse the lump in the porridge with the lump in the breast." Recognize the small things for what they truly are and conserve your strength for the really big issues in life.

As someone who always had difficulty achieving this balance, I now follow a simple rule given to me by a traditional healer in Cape Town, South Africa: empower yourself by only acting in ways that will empower others. Even if you're angry, she told me, act in a way that would make you proud of yourself afterwards. Ultimately, whatever we do to others, we really do to ourselves. Makes you think doesn't it?

No matter who you are, you are accountable. Say it. Live it. Love it. "Business Leaders Face A Grassroots Demand For a Lot Less Hubris" (*Wall Street Journal*, 03/09/04) Arrogance is out of fashion in the executive suite. So are autocratic executives who rule by intimidation, think they have all the answers and don't believe they need to be accountable to anyone.

"Directors and shareholders are rising up and taking power from management. It's a significant shift," says Richard Koppes, of counsel at Jones, Day, Reavis & Pogue in Sacramento, California, and a director at three public companies. It also signals "the generational shift that is occurring – from the imperial, all-powerful, captain-of-the-ship executive to a new kind of CEO who is willing to share authority and be more accountable." Executives who don't demonstrate those qualities may find themselves passed over for the top job. At a time when several former omnipotent CEOs face possible jail sentences, hubris is no longer seen as a strength. CEOs today need a strong sense that they are working for others. They can't direct what a board does, but rather must include members in decision making. At many companies, such as GE, directors are required to visit offices and plants to talk privately to employees.

CEOs also have to provide much more transparency to investors, giving details about financial results they wouldn't have released in the past, and showing they are open to communication and to receiving ideas.

Ken Freeman, CEO of Quest Diagnostics, says leaders must always put the company's needs ahead of their egos. For him, that means building a strong management bench and offering a solid succession plan that addresses a growing company's changing needs. "I'm young and don't want to go yet," Mr. Freeman admits. "But your true legacy as a CEO is what happens to the company after you leave office."

You may not be a CEO of your own company, but you are the CEO of your own Personal Brand. The same rules that apply to Captains of Industry apply to anyone who wants to perform at their Personal Best and help others do the same. **So make humility, accountability, transparency, inclusiveness and service-mindedness part of your repertoire of values.**

Major-General Lewis MacKenzie, now retired, who commanded UN troops during the Bosnian civil war of 1992, summed up the power of accountability with the following powerful comment in the *National Post* (03/22/04):

> For the past 10 years, I have asked the same question of some 300 plus audiences totaling at least a million attendees: "May I have a show of hands please – in your entire life, can you recall one instance where you thought less of a person, no matter what the circumstances, when that individual said, 'I'm responsible'?" I'm still waiting for the first hand to go up.

Makes you think, doesn't it?

The price of Authenticity is mistakes, lots of them.

If that's the case, you may be thinking, why should you even be authentic when caution and reserve may offer better protection against missteps and wrong turns? Simply because our greatest regrets are ALWAYS the things we should have done but never did. It's always the things we omitted, not committed, that cause us the deepest pain. Think about your life: what are the things that you truly regret?

What's more, in turbulent times, fortune favours the person who takes action. The more shots you take at a moving target, the more likely you are to hit it. The headline from the *Globe and Mail Report On Business* (03/16/2001) said it all: "Market gyrations leave strategists clueless." The article goes on to state, "Frankly, it amounts to a pooling of ignorance – strategists manipulating the estimates of analysts who are following the guidelines of managements who are clueless about the course of earnings."

In fact, those people who actually think they do know what's going on are probably living in denial. Welcome to the world of make-it-up-as-we-go-along where Spontaneity rules and Resilience is the prerequisite for sustained success. Seriously, it's your ability to keep coming back from setbacks and wrong turns that will ultimately determine your long-term personal success.

Remember, even monkeys fall out of trees.

Authenticity equals Speed.

While no one truly knows what's going on any more, the one thing we know with absolute certainty is that the future belongs to those people who can adjust and adapt instantly to their changing environment. Authentic people are congruent people – their thoughts and actions coincide exactly with each other. They may be wrong sometimes, but they are never tentative. They know that he who waivers can never win.

There's another huge benefit that comes from increased authentic activity: you learn far more by doing than you ever will by just thinking, speculating and theorizing. You and I can read about something and understand it on an intellectual level. But when we attempt to apply it ourselves, it becomes real.

Action builds our mental muscle. It massively enhances understanding. So step up now. Go and do something before you're ready to do it, because that's the most powerful way to become ready to do it. If you wait until you think you're ready, you'll just be an observer. Get out of the grandstands into the game. Be a player.

Play the game called "Your Life" by your rules.

I enjoy watching people party for two reasons: firstly, I enjoy watching people have a good time. Secondly, I am fascinated by the impact of even a single glass of Chardonnay or Merlot on someone's behaviour. In a heartbeat, they can go from shy and diffident to gregarious and bold. The alcohol dissolves their inhibitions as they reveal more and more of themselves to the audience around them. Of course, the smart ones know when to stop.

Why do most of us need an external agent to set us free? The answer is highly personal to each reader. Culture also plays a role. Without stereotyping, an Italian or American is more likely to be expressive than a Japanese or a Finn. Weather also plays a major role. Toronto or Minneapolis residents are far more likely to loosen up in July than in January. If you know that your culture, your weather conditions or your social conditioning inhibits you from embracing authenticity, you have to be even more aware and courageous in going against the flow to embrace it.

For many of us, it's the simple fear of looking stupid or being humiliated in front of others that stops us from being authentic. We care so much about what others think of us that the pain of rejection or ridicule obliterates whatever pleasure we think we may gain by being authentic. However, if you knew how little time other people spend thinking about you, you wouldn't worry what they think about you. What's more, those that matter won't mind. And those that mind won't matter.

If you play the game called "Your Life" by other people's rules, you cannot be truly happy because you're playing by the wrong rules. There is an Authentic Way for each of us. We have to find it and we have to live it. In your heart, you know what it is for you. Everything begins with a tiny step. Take it today.

The higher the caliber of people I research, the greater their fear of failure or rejection.

It's called the Impostor Syndrome. An impostor is someone who pretends to be what he is not. And many of us are scared that one day someone is going to discover that we're not that clever, or that we're not that charming. So we assume the persona we believe other people will accept; we hold part of ourselves back; we establish a personal buffer zone to protect our vulnerabilities, and we lose both our spontaneity and our joie de vivre.

The irony is that we're really so much more powerful than we give ourselves credit for. There is so much magic that atrophies though simple lack of use. If we did allow people to look more closely at the real us, they would be drawn irresistibly towards us – not be driven away.

I meet so many people who rob others of their magic by keeping it hidden. Whatever the reason, they're afraid to let it out. Perhaps they just don't believe they even have the magic; maybe someone in their past degraded them; maybe someone hurt or humiliated them – a parent, teacher or even a peer. So never underestimate the power of a single statement to scar someone permanently. Sticks and stones may break your bones, but words can wound you forever.

Marianne Williamson expressed the power of authenticity beautifully in her book, *A Return to Love*:

> We ask ourselves, who am I to be brilliant, gorgeous, talented, fabulous? Actually, who are you NOT to be? Your playing small does not serve the world. There is nothing enlightened about shrinking so that other people won't feel insecure around you. As we let our own light shine, we unconsciously give other people permission to do the same. As we are liberated from our own fear, our presence automatically liberates others.

Think about the last time you were with someone who was truly authentic. Didn't she help everyone in the room lighten up? Didn't she boost the energy levels of the entire group? Didn't you feel invigorated? So liberate yourself to be yourself. Once again, this takes courage. It also means flying in the face of conventional wisdom that says: *look before you leap. Don't let people know what you're truly thinking. Don't be vulnerable. Be on your guard. Behave like an adult. Be careful whom you trust. Act responsibly. Don't be transparent. Don't act in haste. Hold your cards close to your chest. Keep your distance and keep your feelings to yourself. Keep a stiff upper lip. Don't let people get too close.*

Conventional wisdom is conventional because it will stop you getting hurt. It offers a sound defensive strategy for those who are afraid of life. Are you afraid of life? Or are you prepared to risk being open? **If you want to thrive, you cannot afford to be a human armadillo. Our Personal Best demands that we open ourselves up to life and to others. Because then life and other people open themselves up to us.**

Put this statement to the test: over the next 48 hours, watch how people respond to people who are stiff, reserved, scared or closed. Then watch how people respond to people who are open, warm, relaxed and confident. You will see that people close down with people who are closed down. They open up to people who have opened up. It's the ultimate law of human energy: like attracts like. Of course, if you're open, you'll get hurt. There's no doubt that someone somewhere sometime will abuse your goodwill. But for every one act of malice, you'll experience multiple acts of reciprocal kindness and generosity.

Accept the offer. Do not block. No wimping.

The ultimate model of Authenticity in action is Improv Comedy. Karyn Bugelli, past Education Coordinator of The Second City in Toronto, expresses the three principles of improv comedy exquisitely when she says:

> Firstly, you need to *Accept The Offer*. You need to accept what the other person is giving you as worthwhile and valid. Accept the offer as reality and without reservation.

> Secondly, *Do Not Block*. Be open. You are there to make the other person look good. Dismantle your preconceptions about the other person or what he should or shouldn't say. Live totally in the moment. Don't worry about the words that may come out of the other person's mouth. Focus fully on what she is saying right now. Listen without bias to one word at a time.

> Thirdly, *No Wimping*. No holding back. Give all you have to whatever you're doing. Invest one hundred per cent of your emotion in your actions. Don't worry about embarrassing yourself. Just play full out. The funniest moments happen when the performer honours his true self. He doesn't go for the cheap laugh. He isn't forcing the humour. Rather, it flows out naturally from his authenticity and desire to make others look and feel good.

More and more, I believe Bugelli's three principles of improv comedy are really the three principles we should all live our lives by. If all you did as a result of this book were accept other's offers unconditionally, open the flow of energy between yourself and others, and stop emotionally wimping out, you would take yourself to the next level.

If, by some remote chance, you're still not convinced of the need to Embrace Authenticity, here's a final reason to buy into it: IT WILL MAKE YOU A LOT OF MONEY! **The golden thread weaving its way through all the great communicators, persuaders and salespeople is their Authentic Enthusiasm for what they're offering their stakeholders. They positively glow with passion for their product or service. Their Spontaneity is infectious. They bypass all the rational blocks of their prospects by going straight to their hearts.**

On the other hand, those people bereft of Authentic Enthusiasm are unconvincing and uninspired. It's important to note here that you do not have to be loud and extroverted to radiate Authentic Enthusiasm. You just have to openly love what you're doing and you have to consciously liberate your authentic self.

Here's a mantra to Authenticity that I carry around with me in my mind. It was given to me by Arca Vigraha Devi Dasi, an eastern mystic I met in Vrindavan, India. I've said it to myself so many times, it's become part of my mental DNA.

> I live in peace and security.
> I surrender all doubt and fear of self.
> I am never limited by past experience or present appearance.
> I bless and let go of all that serves me no more.
> I dare to dream anew.
> I choose what rings true for me.
> And I honor it with love and acceptance.
> I shed every thought separating me from it.
> And finally, I rest secure in the truth that sets me free.
> I can be all that I can and choose to be.

Being You means being idealistic. Being idealistic means being realistic.

The *Webster's Dictionary* defines Idealism as: *the cherishing or pursuit of high or noble principles, purposes or goals.* By this definition, one of the highest principles you can cherish is Yourself — to be all that you can and choose to be. Without this personal idealism, Being-You will stay out of reach.

What other noble principles, purposes or goals do you cherish? Here are some of mine:

I cherish the freedom to be the best me I can be.
I cherish people of honor, action and caring.
I cherish generosity, kindness, spontaneity, daring and courage.
I cherish tenacity, endurance and stamina.
I cherish the look in people's eyes when they're having a breakthrough.
I cherish laughter, joy, passion and confidence.
I cherish my ability to grow and to grow others.
I cherish my connection with magical people.
I cherish youth in people of all ages.
I cherish the feeling of achievement and self-fulfillment.
I cherish making a difference and having a difference made to me.
I cherish the differences in the people around me.
I cherish Canada, what it stands for and what it has offered my family and me.

Being idealistic doesn't mean distancing yourself from the realities of life. On the contrary, it's your idealism that will help you master your realities. Idealism has a luster to it that shines for miles around. If you want to know whether someone has it, look into his eyes. The idealists' eyes are incandescent. 19 or 90, you'll find the look of wonder and possibility. You'll also sense a sharpness and alertness about him that his more cynical counterparts cannot match.

Idealism is in. Cynicism is out. Because cynicism is both the easy and the expected thing to do. There are too many cynics wandering around on the streets. They're not building anything. They're too busy telling you why it can't be done.

If you're an idealist, everything is always possible. Your idealism is like a Teflon skin – nothing can stick to you and nothing can corrupt your trust in yourself and others.

It's called Naïve Experience. It's the unique ability to distill the best of what's happened to you while letting go of the worst. It's the refusal to let your passion wilt under pressure. It's Bob Dylan's secret of remaining "Forever Young":

> *May God bless and keep you always,*
> *May your wishes all come true,*
> *May you always do for others*
> *And let others do for you.*
> *May you build a ladder to the stars*
> *And climb on every rung,*
> *May you stay forever young,*
>
> *May you grow up to be righteous,*
> *May you grow up to be true,*
> *May you always know the truth*
> *And see the lights surrounding you.*
> *May you always be courageous,*
> *Stand upright and be strong,*
> *May you stay forever young,*
>
> *May your hands always be busy,*
> *May your feet always be swift,*
> *May you have a strong foundation*
> *When the winds of changes shift.*
> *May your heart always be joyful,*
> *May your song always be sung,*
> *May you stay forever young.*

These words are more appropriate in 2004 than they were when they first penned in 1974. Every time I conclude one of my sessions with these words, I see the eyes in front of me misting up. In every adult's heart, there is a yearning for the pure ideals of honour, faith, truth, courage, strength, contribution and joy.

The difference between the few and the many is that for the many it's just a song. For the few it's how they live. And you? **Are you *always* in search of wonder and possibility? Or is the cynicism calcifying around you?** Sometimes, though, in an increasingly schizophrenic environment, cynicism must co-exist with idealism. Cynicism can act as a protective barrier as long as it's porous enough to allow delight and surprise in.

Resist the Conformity Vortex. Be Courageous.

Unlike our fellow mammals, in the human kingdom, there isn't safety in numbers. Being part of the herd is not a guarantee of safety.

The more you conform, the more vulnerable you become. The less visible you are, the less you will be missed.

So resist the Conformity Vortex. In every organization I have worked with over the past eighteen months, the call has been for people who were willing to be different, to try different things and take a different path.

"Two roads diverged in a wood, and I took the one less traveled by, and that has made all the difference." Robert Frost

Dr. David Jamieson, head of the Environics Advanced Analytics Unit, states that those people who will thrive in the 2000s have two primary characteristics: a low need for external validation and highly developed internal structure.

In other words, they're willing to back themselves against the resistance of others. And while they like praise and recognition, they're willing to forego them in pursuit of their goals. They also have a tried and tested personal way of processing their thoughts that consistently empowers them. Over time, they have learnt to trust themselves even when nobody else does.

Remember, all progress happens because someone somewhere made the gutsy call against all odds. In fact, **that's how the *Webster's Dictionary* defines the very meaning of courage: *the quality of mind or spirit that enables one to face difficulty, danger and pain with*** *firmness; to act in accordance with one's beliefs in spite of criticism.*

The best teams are filled with individualistic idealists.

The world needs more individualists and it needs more idealists. It needs more people who believe they can change it for the better. Their spirit is summed up by a line from Steven Spielberg's movie, *Schindler's List*: "Whoever saves one life, saves the world entire."

If you're lucky, you have these kinds of people around you right now. I have. Michael Adams. Derek Ruston. Erica Cerny. Hilary Lipkin. Brian Blosser. Martin Perelmuter. Catherine Bridgman. To name a few. Chances are you've never heard of these folk. You have your own band of individualistic idealists around you. Expand it. Treat each member of this band as your most valuable asset. Do whatever it takes to continually enhance your relationship with them.

"You have to be a heck of an individual to play on our team." **Reg Lascaris**

Here's a piece of counter intuitive wisdom: the best teams are filled with individualistic idealists because these individuals back themselves but do what's best for the team. They have personal autonomy and peer accountability in equal measure.

Think about all the best teams you've watched or been in. Think about the members of those teams. Weren't they all characters in their own right? All the best teams I encounter are filled with a cast of characters that would dazzle Scorsese or Spielberg.

Embracing Authenticity means learning how to be vulnerable.

I learnt the real power of being vulnerable on a recent flight from Johannesburg to Cape Town in South Africa. Just before the doors of the aircraft closed, a blind man was ushered into the seat next to me. I saw him reach into his bag and pull out a brail publication. Then I observed him eat his meal in the close confines of a coach-class seat.

Most importantly, I watched the way everyone around him tried extra hard to make his life a little easier. There was an extraordinary air of serenity and self-assurance about him, as though he knew the world would give him whatever he needed exactly when he needed it. I asked him what he was reading. "*National Geographic*," he replied, following up with an enquiry as to who I was and what I did. We began talking and he told me that he was Dr. William Rowland, head of the South African National Council for the Blind.

Having established a rapport with William, I asked him about his primary strategy for thriving as a blind person in a seeing world. "It's simple," he replied. "I'm dependent on everybody. And because I'm dependent on everyone, I not only have to trust them, I have to continually ask them for help in a way that you don't have to. And you know what? I've never been taken advantage of, and people almost always give me the help I ask for."

Which just goes to show that sometimes, the more dependent you are on others, the more interdependent you become. Now, I'm not suggesting that you continually lean on others to support you. I AM suggesting that you stop being afraid to lean on them when you're not strong. If you've surrounded yourself with the right people, they'll consider it a compliment to be asked for their help and support.

Time after time, managers tell me that their biggest human resource difficulties are caused by people who are afraid to ask for help because they don't want to appear weak. So they struggle ineffectually with the problem until it becomes so big that they are forced to get help. By that stage, however, it's grown to Godzilla-sized proportions and the energy required to resolve it is quadrupled.

Nothing is more likely to annoy your colleagues or customers than being given unnecessary trouble. Although people may sometimes complain about unforeseen hassles, in the main they accept them as inevitable, everyday parts of life. What they will not accept are problems that could easily have been avoided by a little honesty and transparency. So if you need help, ask for it now!

I want to finish this chapter with a quote from Leo Buscaglia, the self-proclaimed Doctor of Love. Just before he died, he delivered a seminar where he began with this poignant statement:

"When you go up to meet your Creator, he only asks you one question: were you you?"

What will your answer be?

**LIVE IN THE
SWEET
SPOT.**

STEP 4:
Play Full Out

Leave Nothing Behind.
FLAP.
Be Worthy Of Your Gifts.

4

Your "Play Full Out" Self-Exploration

Here is a simple 10 point test to determine your command of this skill. For each question, rate yourself on a scale of 1-10.

- ☐ • I always play to win
- ☐ • I always follow through on my promises
- ☐ • I have a great amount of vigor and vitality
- ☐ • I have deep endurance and stamina
- ☐ • I take care of my body through the right food and exercise
- ☐ • Other people are attracted to my energy
- ☐ • I live each day as though it could be my last
- ☐ • I prepare myself thoroughly for every meeting
- ☐ • I honour my intuition by listening to my instincts
- ☐ • I feel young mentally and physically

○ total

- **If you scored between 85 and 100**
Congratulations. You're already "Playing Full Out."
- **If you scored between 70 and 84**
You're still holding something back.
- **If you scored less than 70**
You're leaving too much behind.
This chapter will help you bring everything you have to everything you do.

Athlete: *1. one trained to compete in contests involving agility, stamina or strength; a trained competitor in a sport, exercise or game requiring skill. 2. one who contends for a prize.* (*Webster's Dictionary*)

So tell me, do you love winning? Do you need the feeling of triumph and fulfillment that comes with victory? Do you want to be Number One? Do you enjoy the kudos that comes with being a star? Do you crave the personal-high of performing like a champion?

How much? Seriously, how much do you need to win? How much do you need to come first? How important is it to you to perform at the peak of your ability? How important is it that you're seen to be the best?

Now, how much do you love to train? Are you prepared to train so hard it hurts? Are you prepared to risk failure, embarrassment, and rejection in the quest for Your Personal Best? Are you willing to give it your all, every opportunity you have? Are you willing to pay the price? Or are you just window-shopping?

In my seminars, I ask people the simple question: how many of you love to win? Of course, everyone raises their hands. Then I ask the question I've just asked you: how many of you love to train so hard it hurts? Less than 10 per cent of people raise their hands. And of those 10 per cent, only 10 per cent really mean it. The One Percenters. And that's why so few people truly experience the nirvana of achieving their Personal Best.

In the long run, there's a direct symmetry between training and achieving Your Personal Best. Training plus talent plus tenacity equals triumph. My metaphor is the Olympic Games. For 100 years, the world's best athletes have competed with each other in this exalted contest. They were born with huge gifts. And yet, they train relentlessly to take their gifts to the highest level.

Well, we're all athletes in the game called life. I'm a writing, speaking, motivating athlete. You may be a sales, accounting, service, administrative or political athlete. But you're a competitor, you're a player, you're a member of a team. And your ultimate success will be a direct function of your commitment to personal development and playing full out.

Think of three people you know who you think always play full out. Maybe you know them personally, or maybe you know them through the media. Write down their names. Now, write down their achievements; write down your feelings towards them; write down what you believe other people feel towards them; write down how you think they feel about themselves. And by the way, would you include yourself on this list of People-Who-Always-Play-Full-Out?

I'll make this prediction: all the people on your Play Full Out list are the most successful people around you. They are the ones who are making the most of their time, their opportunities and their resources. They are the ones with guts and grit. They're the fighters and the finishers. They're the ones who rally others to their cause.

Three out of four people around you have lost their Mojo.

In 1996, the Environics 3SC Social Values Research indicated that 39% of Canadians were focused on personal development. They invested in themselves. They sought personal fulfillment through a lifestyle combining experimentation and well-being. They were open to the influence of others and considered social contact an enriching experience. They were committed to personal vitality and pursued self-expression.

By the end of 2002, that percentage had more than halved to 19 per cent. Natural crises, terrorism, the dot.com bomb, the stock-market meltdown, corporate downsizing, outsourcing of jobs, and the accelerating velocity of change all combined to massively increase people's fear of the future. Fall and winter replaced spring and summer. In the age of *Apocalyptic Anxiety*, personal survival supplanted personal development.

A year later, by the end of 2003, the percentage of Canadians committed to personal development had rebounded to 26 per cent, a remarkable resurgence from 2002 but still dramatically down from 1996.

Even when it comes to technology, Canadians are becoming fatigued. Canada has the highest percentage of the population in the world linked to the Internet. And yet, Environics has noted a dramatic decline in a trend called *Enthusiasm for Technology*. This trend is defined as: *a favourable bias toward technology; a tendency to be fascinated with the possibilities offered by modern technology; to believe that technology is the best tool for facing today's world, one that helps us adapt and respond to the demands of daily life.*

From 1996 to 2003, Enthusiasm for Technology declined by 27 per cent. The myth of the technological panacea is vaporizing. There is no machine that can soothe the soul.

In North America, the fear of the future is a remarkably

democratic angst, affecting everyone from the cashier to the CEO. For the past seven years, PricewaterhouseCoopers, one of the world's leading professional service firms, has surveyed 1400 CEOs in 40 countries to better understand and anticipate the critical issues facing the global economy. The 2004 survey – perhaps the most comprehensive view of how companies see the risks they face – reveals an interesting trend: U.S. CEOs are less optimistic than their counterparts in other parts of the world. More than two thirds (68%) believe the current environment is making companies risk averse. Only five per cent of U.S. CEOs say they are significantly more aggressive in their attitude towards risk taking.

What is this socio-quake telling us?

Three out of four people are struggling to regain their personal vitality and stamina. They're being worn away from within. Too much is happening too quickly. There is a permanent feeling of being out of control. In all our research with people across the continent, people tell us that they're losing their bearings. Just when they thought they had slain one monster, another rises to take its place. Burnout is just a heartbeat away.

As you look around you, know that only one out of four people are your real competitors. They're the ones whose Mojo keeps growing. They understand nature's fundamental law: if you're not busy growing, you're busy dying. And by that law, many people around you are busy dying. In fact, many may never have even lived.

Across the U.S. and Canada, I see people on permanent-pause. They're stuck in "no-man's land." What do I mean? They believe they could be doing better. They believe they could perform at a higher level. They believe their life could be more rewarding. But they also believe things could be a heck of a lot worse. They're focusing on what could go wrong, not on the extraordinary rewards that accrue to being Best-In-Class. In other words, they're not playing to win. They're playing not to lose. And that's a one-way ticket to mediocrity.

I'm not telling you to be reckless here. I'm not telling you to abandon your caution. There's too much at stake to be cavalier. **I am asking you to bring all of yourself to everything you do. I'm asking you to focus on what you can do, not what you cannot. I'm asking you to be decisive, not ambivalent.**

And by the way, when people tell you they're skeptical or cynical about something, what they're really telling you is that they're scared. They're afraid to commit themselves to a course of action in case they fail or become disappointed. They're giving themselves an escape clause even before they've embarked on their journey. Skepticism and cynicism will make the mind septic. Avoid them at all costs.

If you want to outplay your competition, play full out. The Goddess of Victory is attracted to Congruence.

Have you ever been in a meeting with someone who may have said all the right things, but you felt as though they didn't mean what they said? Ever known someone who didn't follow through on their promises? Ever felt like someone just wasn't telling you the truth? Ever felt like someone was holding something back from you? Ever felt frustrated because someone just wouldn't commit to a course of action?

All the time, right? These are examples of incongruence. And they're the norm, not the exception. They're the symptoms of hesitation and uncertainty. They're also contagious. If you're near incongruence, you tend to catch it. We become the company that we keep.

On the other hand, here's **Lipkin's definition of Congruence:** *consistency between what you say and what you do; the vitality to stay the course; determination to convert potential into achievement; commitment to always being Your Personal Best; desire to help others be the most they can be; willingness to go first; need to be great every day; possession of the stamina to hang in when others have let go; representation of certainty in the face of uncertainty.*

By that definition, how congruent are you? Think about this one carefully because **your congruence will be the biggest single reason for your success over the next twelve months. Congruence and decisiveness are Siamese twins. The more congruent you are, the more decisions you make. The more decisions you make, the better you become at making decisions. The better your decisions, the better your actions. And the better your actions, the better your results.** And the better your results, the higher your level of motivation to do more, and more, and more.

Here's a Lipkin newsflash: your success is never a matter of IQ. It's always a matter of congruence. If you can understand these words, you've got enough intellectual horsepower to get what you want. The real question is: what are you prepared to do to get what you want? And are you prepared to keep on doing it, through setback after setback?

In the game of life, it's not about who's right; it's about who's left. Visceral Vitality is the real currency of achievement.

Environics/Lipkin defines *Visceral Vitality* as: *The ability to sustain a 24/7/365 level of enormous animation, liveliness and health; a deep well of internal emotional, mental and physical personal reserves that you can draw on at any time; when you feel as though you're living with every iota of your personal power; when you exist fully in the moment, totally absorbed in the person directly in front of you, or the task at hand; when you feel fully alive with physical vigor and health; when you're living in alignment with your values and in harmony with yourself; when, to quote F. Scott Fitzgerald, you feel "a heightened sensitivity to the promises of life."*

In a 24/7 world, your mind will only get you so far. Caffeine may get you a little further. But our research says there is one primary quality that is the defining trait of high achievers: Visceral Vitality. It's your Visceral Vitality that will really empower you to stay the course.

There are lots of people with great ideas. There are also many who start applying their ideas. They begin the game well. Then, as the setbacks, rejections, and misfires take their toll, they back off from their dreams – fatigued and frustrated.

In Africa, one of nature's most powerful predators is the cheetah. The cheetah can reach speeds of up to 120km/hr. It's a hunting machine, superbly designed for its craft. And yet, do you know how often a cheetah misses its prey? Nine times out of ten! Imagine what would happen to the cheetah if on the ninth miss, it exclaimed: "Enough of this, I think I'll become a vegetarian!"

The cheetah can't just give up and yield to burnout. The cheetah has no choice. He has to persevere if he wants to eat. And so he does. Stopping the hunt is not an option open to his psyche. It's the same with the best human hunters. They have the vitality to persevere until they get their desired result.

It's extraordinary how low down Vitality is on the list of many people's values. They're so busy just surviving that boosting their vitality fits somewhere between impossibility and a dream. Look around you. How many people radiate an energy that actually energizes you?

How many people look as though they're living a great life? It's ironic – **Vitality, the one quality that drives all peak performance, is the one that is most neglected by the vast majority of people.** In fact, in the pursuit of results, vitality is often the first casualty. Stress, overwork, anxiety, and overindulgence are the nemesis of Playing-Full-Out.

So how serious are you about your vitality? What are you doing right now to enhance your personal energy? Are you living in the Loser's Land of "I should" or has Visceral Vitality become an absolute non-negotiable in your life? You're on an exercise program, right? You eat foods that cleanse you, not clog you, right? You spend time with people who "juice" you, right? You feed your mind with literature that inspires you, right? You consciously sustain an optimistic state of mind, right? You live a life consistent with your values, right? You would never consciously do anything that would pollute your internal reserves of energy, right? You have regular check-ups to determine the health of your physical machine, right?

Perhaps you're one of the lucky ones who have been born with a surplus of vitality and a body that can withstand any punishment. Maybe you're one of those rare human beings who can sustain a relentless pace without rest or recreation. Even so, it's just a matter of time before you pay the price for your neglect. Consider this a gentle reminder

The quality of your play determines the quality of your work. All work and no play makes you blind, blunt and boring. Without a break, you will break. You have to be a part-time hedonist. But unless your playtime prepares you for the next professional challenge, it diminishes you.

What am I saying here? Beware of the desire for total distraction. My friend Dr. Bernard Levinson calls it "The hunt for oblivion." Food, drink, drugs, TV, shopping and mindless pursuits may anesthetize you for the moment, but they don't enhance you for the next challenge.

Choose your poison carefully. There's a big difference between relaxation and re-creation. Too much relaxation makes you slack, sloppy and slothful. Re-creation, on the other hand, is not about distraction. It's about getting traction for the next encounter with the unknown.

Re-creation is the essential vaccine against fatigue and overwhelm. It's the recharging of the spirit, renewal of the mind and rejuvenation of the body. It's sparkling dialogue with effervescent people; it's the burn and the sweat from a great workout; it's the quiet time in your mind; it's seven hours of deep uninterrupted sleep; it's a subtle Shiraz or a smooth Scotch; it's a turquoise ocean or a white capped peak; it's Robert De Niro or Salma Hayek; it's William Styron or Jane Urquhart; it's Eric Clapton or BB King; it's smoked salmon or seared tuna; it's sharing and intimacy with your soulmate.

Those are some of my favourite things. That's how I psyche myself for the next round of challenges. How about you?

Visceral Vitality will be your sharpest competitive edge.

Unless you own skills that provide you with a personal monopoly, or unless you're someone who has already achieved all you want to achieve in material terms, the reality is that you are operating in an increasingly competitive environment where all your competitors have access to the same information. All your competitors are smart. All your competitors are damn good, otherwise they wouldn't even have lasted this long. All your competitors are getting better. So what's the mark of the winners? They are those players who can do the most with the least. The further the game goes, the better they do. They recover faster, they last longer, they think more clearly, they lead better, they inspire more strongly – they are the human Energizer bunnies, lasting up to five times longer than ordinary humans.

People with Visceral Vitality are the ones who are most in demand in a continual do-more-with-less marketplace. And they are the rare minority. **In almost all the briefings I have received from management teams across the U.S. and Canada, their number one desire was not greater talent or commitment, it was "upbeat stick-to-itiveness."** This is the ability not just to stay the course, but also to do so with demonstrable gusto and vigor.

One of my favourite true stories of all time about stick-to-itiveness is about Steven Bradbury who won the men's 1000 metre short-track event at the 2002 Salt Lake City Olympics (*Globe and Mail* 02/18/02):

> The luckiest man at the Winter Olympics is an Australian speed skater who once sliced his leg open and almost bled to death on the ice only to recover and break his neck.
>
> In the men's 1000 metre short-track event, everybody fell down and Mr. Bradbury won. It happened in the quarter-final, in the semi-final and it happened again, for the third time on the same night, on the last corner in the final. Everybody fell down and Mr. Bradbury won.
>
> Short-trackers have a habit of falling down and taking each other out like pins in a bowling alley. But what happened for Mr. Bradbury was beyond anything that anyone had ever seen before. In the final, Mr. Bradbury was so far behind his rivals he could have stopped and asked for directions. He looked like a guy trying to hail a cab. Then all of a sudden China's Li Jiajun went down. Then Korea's Hyun-Soo

Ahn went down and took out Mr. Ohno and Mr. Turcotte, and Mr. Bradbury cruised past thinking, "Hang on. This can't be right. I think I won."

Mr. Bradbury's career has produced as many near-death experiences as accomplishments. At a 1994 World Cup event in Montreal, he slipped and impaled his right thigh on a skate blade. The gash was so severe he lost four litres of blood and required 111 stitches. He said he would have died if it hadn't been for the fast work of the paramedics who treated him.

Then in 2000, he fell while training in Australia and crashed headfirst into a barrier, breaking the C4 and C5 vertebrae in his neck. For six weeks he wore a metal halo.

But even after two horrific injuries, Mr. Bradbury refused to pass on a sport that had taken him to the 1992, 1994 and 1998 Winter Games. Instead, he wanted one last go at the Olympics so he could "walk away satisfied." Never in his wildest dreams did he expect to walk away as an Olympic champion, the guy who stayed on his feet when everyone else was skating on banana peels; Australia's new Olympic hero, whose brilliant strategy was to stay behind the leaders in case they fell down.

Yup, in order to finish first, you must first finish.

FLAP — Finish Like a Pro.

Step up when others are winding down. You define yourself through your conduct in the final moments. Watch people in the closing stages of a meeting or assignment. Most of the time, there's a visible fall off in energy and application.

It's all about endurance. Maybe that's why it's the number one quality of CEOs worldwide. I've had the great privilege of working with a number of great CEOs around the world. In every single case, their edge has been their ability to sustain focus and judgment without becoming fatigued. What's more, it's their virtually boundless energy that is the trait that most impresses the rest of their team. In many cases, the CEOs legendary stamina alone earns them the right to lead. Everyone can be outstanding at the beginning of the game. Only those with Visceral Vitality are even better at the end. Are you?

Whatever your position, you are solely responsible for your own life, so what's your strategy for boosting your vitality? There is no quick fix. There's no pill nor doctor's scalpel that can give you sustained Visceral Vitality. It must become a religious part of your daily or weekly regimen.

The Dalai Lama is the ultimate model of Visceral Vitality. When he is travelling, according to the *Globe and Mail* (04/10/04), he often has a schedule of meetings nothing short of grinding: one day in Melbourne, for example, he had 17 appointments, beginning with a rabbi at 7:50 a.m. and ending with an evening lecture to 20 000 people titled "Inner Peace, World Peace." His performance is fuelled by his strict regimen of meditation, diet, scriptural reading, exercise, conversation, mantras and prayer. And by the way, compared to his workload, how's your job looking?

Sustaining Visceral Vitality is not a chore; it's a series of activities designed to stimulate heart, mind and body. The challenge for all of us is to design a strategy that's right for us. What may work for the Dalai Lama or Mike Lipkin may be totally inappropriate for you. Only you know what's right for you, and only you can take action. Do it. For once in your life, put yourself first. Design a personal program that fits your life and your challenges.

You'll be amazed at how easy it is. I promise that you can find the time just by eliminating all the non-value adding activities that are cannibalizing your vitality right now. I'm talking about all those things you do when you're putting off what you know you really have to do. **Avoid dis-traction. Get traction.**

You HAVE to find the time because boosting your Visceral Vitality will help you do so much more with your time. Hey, try it for six months. If you don't see a noticeable difference in the quality of your life, go back to the way you were. There's no downside here. Take action and follow through – because, at the end of the day, there are only two kinds of people in this world: those that make it happen and those that wonder what happened.

Life is the ultimate marathon. It isn't over until it's over. Thomas Meehan, 72, Broadway's hottest writer and creator of *Annie*, *Hairspray* and *The Producers*, is the poster boy for sustained perseverance. At 45, he wrote *Annie*. Then he had to wait 25 years before he penned *The Producers* and *Hairspray*. As Meehan puts it, "I'm proof that things can happen late in the game and keep on happening. That's what all my shows are about: underdogs getting what they want in the end." No matter how old you are, you can get what you want, if you play full out.

It's only too late if you don't begin NOW.

For boomers like myself, who are reading these words, there is increasing evidence that a careful regimen of exercise and diet can stave off the ageing process significantly. No matter how talented you are, you cannot perform if you don't train. You cannot play at your best if you are not physically at your best. Look at yourself in the mirror. Do you like what you see? Are you at or near your optimal shape, weight and fitness? Or are you carrying unnecessary pounds that may not only slow you down, but also take you out of the game completely?

According to *Time* Magazine (02/05/01), over the past five years, scientists have reached a heartening conclusion: the body has an amazing ability to heal itself. "At any time you decide to improve your behaviour and make lifestyle changes, they make a difference from that point on," says Dr. Jeffrey Koplan, director of the Centers for Disease Control. "Maybe not right away. It's like slamming on the brakes. You do need a certain skid distance." But the skid distance can be remarkably short. Consider these astounding dispatches from the front lines of medical research:

- Women who consume as little as 225g of fish a week cut their risk of suffering a stroke almost in half.
- Eating more fruits, vegetables and fibre changes the blood's sensitivity to insulin within two weeks, helping decrease the risk of diabetes almost immediately.
- Hitherto sedentary 40-year-old women who start walking briskly for half an hour a day, four days a week, enjoy almost the same low risk of heart attack as women who have exercised conscientiously their entire lives.
- The day you quit smoking, the carbon monoxide levels in your body drop dramatically. Within a week, your blood becomes less sticky and your risk of dying suddenly from a heart attack begins to decline. Four to five years later, the chance you will have a heart attack falls to almost the level of someone who has never smoked.

Adopting healthy habits won't cure all that ails you, of course. But doctors believe that as many as 70 per cent of all chronic diseases in the U.S., from diabetes and high blood pressure to heart disease and even some cancers, can be warded off with some timely, sensible changes in lifestyle. Unfortunately, undoing the damage from a lifestyle of bad habits means learning – and sticking with – a whole new set of behaviours. After all, anybody can lose 5kg, and many of us have – over and over again. It's only by maintaining that weight loss, however, that you derive real, lasting benefits.

The good news is that even small changes can lead to big improvements. Not sure where to start? Surprisingly, it doesn't really matter, since one positive change usually leads to another. Becoming more active physically, for example, inspires many people to eat a healthier diet. Make enough changes, and eventually you'll discover you've adopted a new way of life. You'll never know how much damage you can undo if you don't try.

What you do know beyond a shadow of a doubt, however, is what will happen if you don't make the changes. So start slowly. Decide on the one most important thing that you're going to do differently and then follow through. Then decide on the next thing and follow through on that. Then the next and the next. What's more, every time you decide on the one thing you're going to do, celebrate it by telling everyone around you that you're going to do it. That way, you can't turn back.

Like it or not, you'd better find a way to love it.

According to the *Globe and Mail* (09/24/03) survey participants from a range of industries across Canada report that, currently, 48 per cent of their employees are 40 and older. By 2013, they expect that 55 per cent of their employees will be 40 and older. And the older you get, the crueler time and gravity becomes. That means Visceral Vitality needs to be pursued with greater and greater vigor.

You can make that pursuit a grudge activity. Or you can make it a labour of love. Over time, we tend to follow our pleasures not our pains. So, whether you're a fan of physical exercise or not, find a way to derive pleasure from it. Find the right form of exercise for you. Listen to the right music or story. Find the right companion at the right time in the right place. And firm up those mental, emotional and physical muscles.

Your Visceral Vitality determines your capacity for opportunities.

The higher your Visceral Vitality, the better you will be at seizing and exploiting opportunities. Our research shows that **the vast majority of people don't miss opportunities because they're not smart enough. They miss them because they don't have enough energy to pursue them.** They believe that just getting through the day is consuming more resources than they already have. So when they're exposed to a potential opportunity, they say to themselves: "It would be nice to do that but, with everything I have on my plate right now, I just can't..." Sound familiar? Yes, you can.

You have no idea how much latent power is lying unused within you. Heed the words of Oscar Wilde when he said, "Most of us take our music with us to the grave." Is that you? Are you saving the most wonderful part of you for the worms? Make a vow right now to yourself that you will recharge your Visceral Vitality and do just one thing to liberate your "music" right now. In fact, let's have some "serious fun." Wherever you are, please raise your right hand and say,

"I solemnly swear, that as a result of these words, I will do whatever it takes to

increase my Visceral Vitality so I can seize my biggest opportunity with passion and power. No excuses."

That's it. You've now made a vow to yourself. Honour it. Don't let yourself down. Share your vow with someone else. Enlist their help in seizing your opportunity.

Do you know people who seem to be able to do it all? Either they seem to have access to a forty-hour day, or they appear to move at double the speed of normal humans. When you're with these kinds of people, don't they seem to be vibrating at a higher frequency? Isn't it as though they literally crackle with energy? Well, these are the folk who are rich in Visceral Vitality. Spend time with them. Ask them how they make so many of their dreams happen. You know what their response will be? They'll look at you, pause for a moment while they're thinking, and then they'll tell you that they don't think they're working any harder than you are. They'll seem almost surprised at the question.

You see, for them, operating out of Visceral Vitality has become instinctive. They wouldn't dream of doing anything that didn't contribute to their mission. **Consciously or unconsciously, they've got into the rhythm of the empowering ritual. Now, just like anyone who has become outstanding at anything, they make it look so easy.** But watch them closely: they never stop doing those things that keep vitalizing them.

Ultimately, it's your level of Visceral Vitality that determines people's desire to be with you.

Think about this question: what are you really to the people around you? Aren't you just a bundle of emotional energy? Through your words, actions and sheer presence, don't you make them feel good or bad? So, how do you make the people around you feel? Are you a vitality-enhancer or a vitality-vampire?

Over 90 per cent of all communication is non-verbal. That means the sound of our voice and our physical appearance and gestures are what truly impact others. So, if I were to listen to your voice, would I hear the tone of turned-on passion and vitality? Or would I hear anxiety — the archenemy of vitality? Or would I just hear the usual tone of neutrality and compliance? And if I looked at you, what would your stance and physiology be? Would I be struck by your aura of confidence and assurance? As I watched you speak, would I say to myself, "My goodness, this person loves what he's doing. He really cares about helping me"? Or would I say to myself, "This person is just going through the motions. He seems a little bored"?

My job is really about sharing my Visceral Vitality with others. Yes, I believe that my content is world class but then, so is the content of hundreds of my competitors. What people really want is a direct high speed connection to energy and enthusiasm. In fact, that's why you're still reading these words. I know that you can feel the heat of my excitement radiating off the page.

Do other people get that sense from you? It doesn't matter whether you're an extrovert or an introvert. Some of the most vital people I know are quiet, softly spoken individuals. But when they look at me I can see the four magical ingredients of Visceral Vitality in their eyes: Intensity, Sincerity, Caring and Conviction. In fact, I believe that if you're naturally shy, you may even have an advantage over more ebullient fellows like me. You know why? Because you're gentle. You engage the trust and confidence of others immediately. Shy people are often the most eloquent people. So, if you are shy, use your shyness to your advantage. Don't hide behind it.

It's all about the 0.19 second advantage. Live by the Law of Disproportionate Reward

In the 2000 Sydney Olympics, Maurice Greene won the 100-meter track event in a world-record time of 9.86 seconds. What did Greene get? Everything – the gold medal, the acclaim, the lucrative sponsorships.

Unless you're a real running aficionado, you don't know that the man who came fourth was Bernard Williams. His time? 10.05 seconds, less than a fifth of a second slower than Greene. But look at the disproportionate reward that accrued to Greene in contrast to Williams. Williams is still the fourth fastest human in the world. But what did he get that day? The memory of having participated.

So I'm not asking you to make a quantum leap forward as a result of reading these words. I know you're already among the best of your breed. All I'm asking is that you enhance your performance by 0.19 seconds. We all know that life isn't fair, so you may as well use its unfairness to your advantage.

I'm writing these words on a fresh Spring 2004 morning in Toronto, Canada. In a world-class city, I'm surrounded by world-class people. I think of my competitors; I think of my clients; I think of my partners. They're all excellent because excellence is the price of entry. Excellence earns you the right to be a candidate.

Success is about taking excellence to the next level — the level of phenomenal, wicked, awesome, record-breaking, superb, unprecedented, knock-your-socks-off, blow-them-

away, slam-dunk, who's-your-daddy-now, gob-smacking, thrilling, you-make-my-heart-sing brilliance.

And the difference between mere excellence and the next level? You guessed it – 0.19 per cent. It's the tiny bit extra that lifts the whole performance into the Magical Zone. You know what I'm talking about. You've been there. It's intoxicating. It's when your every point is delivered with power and grace; it's when your words are infused with an insight and clarity that mesmerizes the people around you; it's when your ideas seem sculpted by a divine power; it's when you're flying in the jet stream of your Personal Best.

So how do you achieve the 0.19 per cent edge? You romance it. You invite it in. You consistently ask yourself how you can embed it in your performance. You experiment. You search for it in others' performance. You seek inspiration everywhere. Where others end, you begin. You never stop asking. You never stop exploring. You never become complacent.

And still that may not be enough. No one hits a home run every time. In fact, no one even hits the ball every time. Despite the fact that I'm writing a book on Personal Consistency, I still have those days when I fail to get into the High-Performance-Zone. While my preparation always ensures I deliver a satisfactory performance, sometimes the Gods of Motivation are not with me. That's just the way it is. By playing full out, however, I ensure that they're with me more often than the competition.

My entire life philosophy in eight words: Sell Each Line As Hard As You Can.

Jerry Seinfeld is a role model for me, not just because he makes me laugh, but also because he always plays full out. On January 3, 2003, Jerry Seinfeld came to Ottawa for a one-night performance where he tested his new material. He's a smart man – he comes north to Canada to test his material so he can still go home if it doesn't work.

At $100 a ticket, the show sold out 4000 seats in 17 minutes. The next morning, Paul Wells of the *National Post* wrote, "I saw not just a very skilled comedian, but by all appearances a serene and well-adjusted man who has returned to his first love with fresh enthusiasm. This Seinfeld came to work: dressed to the nines in a suit; pacing the stage restlessly; selling each line as hard as he could. He has returned to the primal root of his craft. He stands in front of a microphone and he tells jokes."

If I watched you at work, could I apply a similar description to the way you go about your business? Do you lean into each line and sell it as hard as you can? If Seinfeld still does it, why not you? It works for him and I promise you it will work for you.

Remember, **the person in front of you doesn't care how many times you've said your words before. This moment is all that matters.** They want to feel as though they are your most important stakeholders. They want to be led. They want to be convinced. So step up. Lean into what you're saying. Sell each line as hard as you can. Finish your statements with a declaration not a question mark.

Think about the people you work with. Think about how few of them present themselves with passion – all the time. Think about how feel about those who do. Become one of them. Practice. Be Aware. Overcome your self-consciousness. Make every interaction an exercise in more forceful communication.

I want to share one of my most rewarding professional experiences with you. In October 2003, I delivered a 45-minute after dinner speech to Unilock, a highly successful Canadian company that manufactures and sells paving stones into both the U.S. and Canadian markets. I was at my Personal Best that evening and the applause was loud and long. But that's not why I'm telling you this story. The reason is a sales representative from Chicago called Kyle Trippeer and here is the e-mail he sent me:

> *Mike,*
> *I want to personally thank you for bringing such energy to the Unilock Sales meeting. I can honestly tell you I don't remember a whole lot of the words you spoke, but what sticks in my mind is the energy that you gave throughout the whole room. I have fed off of your energy and used it in many situations in my own life. No, I am not going to tell you how the 45min speech you gave changed my life forever, but I will tell you that I know now in every situation I am in, I can give 100% of my energy and my point will come across. In the past I have held back a little for fear of intimidating someone and still have been successful, but using my unlimited amount of determination, I feel no limit to my success at work or home. I can only hope other Unilock employees were able to take from you what I have. ENERGY. Hope to see you again in the future.*
>
> *Kyle Trippeer*
> *Unilock Chicago*

Kyle epitomizes the essence of Playing Full Out. He is ENERGY in motion. All I did was help him give himself permission to bring all of himself to every meeting.

And by the way, here's the real reason why you should be like Kyle and give 100 per cent of your energy: you don't know how much time you have. I don't make this point to alarm you. I simply make it to remind you that no one has an infinite supply of tomorrows. So **if today were your last day, wouldn't you want it** to be the best day you've ever had? Act every day like it's your last day, and your actions will become your legacy.

Beware of "Surfer's Voice." Switch off in order to Switch on.

I know you've heard it. It's the new wave of inattention. It's called "Surfer's Voice" – the habit of half-heartedly talking to someone on the telephone while simultaneously surfing the Web, reading e-mails, or trading instant messages. It goes something like "OK...uh-hum...right...hmmm" and it's punctuated with surreptitious tapping of a keyboard.

The *Wall Street Journal* calls it "Absent Presence." We're there but we're not. We're so habituated into "Multi-channeling" that we're finding tougher and tougher to concentrate on any one thing at a time. The result is a drifting and diffusion of our energy. Well, just as Jerry Seinfeld and Kyle Trippeer invest all their energy in their engagements, invest all your energy in every telephone conversation.

Multitasking has become the mantra of a culture that possesses the power and the desire to do many things at once. But that technology-charged impatience has a fatal flaw. According to the *Globe and Mail* (02/02/02), researchers are showing that when you do two or more activities at once, your performance invariably suffers. Cognitive scientists call it inattentional blindness or deafness.

David Strayer, a professor of psychology at the University of Utah, discovered something fascinating: in comparing cell phone use while driving with being legally drunk, the drunks are better drivers. When he put 21 cell phone-using subjects on his driving simulator, three of them had accidents. But when he switched to people who exceeded the 0.8 blood-alcohol level that is a commonly used standard of intoxication, none of the seven people he tested on the simulator had an accident. Makes you think, doesn't it?

You can't play full out unless you're fully engaged. Switch off in order to switch on. Unless you need your computer to review data while you're on the phone, turn it off or turn it away. The other person can hear immediately when you lose attention. And it annoys them. Instead, become known as a Terrific Telephone Conversationalist. Make every call a virtuoso performance. You'll be rewarded by receiving a lot more of them.

Do you have BGT? Get it in advance by being Performance-Ready.

Visceral Vitality, to paraphrase Vince Lombardi, is not a some-time thing; it's an all-the-time thing. So how are you on a Monday morning, after a heavy weekend? What's your personal morale like in the middle of February after a solid month of sleet, ice and snow? And what is your mood like after a defeat? How's your energy level at the end of an intense day?

Do you have a deliberate strategy for accessing your Visceral Vitality exactly when you need it? Most importantly, do you have BGT – that's Big Game Temperament? Are you the one who gets the final play in the final minute in the final quarter because your team-members know you'll carry it off?

I call this the **Vinatieri Factor:** A mastermind praised for his preparation, New England Patriots Coach, Bill Belichick, was ready for an all too familiar situation when Carolina tied the 2004 Super Bowl with 68 seconds left. Tom Brady moved the ball into field-goal position, and Adam Vinatieri kicked a 41-yarder with four seconds left to give New England a 32-29 victory against the Panthers – the Patriots' second NFL title in three years.

"If you've got to have one kick with the game on the line, he's the one I'd want kicking them," Belichick said. "That was the game. That's what Adam's here for."

Vinatieri's final kick was all the more remarkable because he missed his first two. But here's how he described the challenge to himself – it's a masterpiece of self-motivation: "That first [kick] I was a little excited. I think I went a little too fast and pushed it right," Vinatieri said. "The next one, Carolina did a nice job ... they got it blocked. But coming out on the third one, I'm kinda thinkin', '*If I hit this one, the other two don't matter,*' so I just tried to do what I could," he said. Beautiful!

From Adam Vinatieri to Alex Rodriquez, the man the *New York Times* calls "the best player in baseball" (*New York Times* 04/04/04). "*I actually enjoy working and honing my game as much as the game itself,*" says Rodriquez, "*if not more. My standards are higher than anybody could ever have on me. Pressure is relative. But I am a big believer that my own type of pressure I put on myself always supersedes anything anyone else might put on me. I like to keep a little pressure, a little tension on my back at all times.*"

Rodriquez said he never wants to let any aspect of his game go bad, so he keeps a mental checklist of areas to work on throughout the season. One day, pop-ups. Another, breaking balls. **Rodriquez breaks down the game into small areas of focus and repeatedly drills himself on them. He knows how talented he is and thrives off the challenge of staying the best.**

Could I say the same about you? Do you know how talented you are and do you thrive off the challenge of staying the best? If Rodriquez invests the kind of energy he does in fine-tuning his skills, why wouldn't you? Natural gifts will only get you so far. Developing them through continuous and never-ending improvement will take you the rest of the way.

Every presentation is like Super Bowl Sunday or the World Series for me. If I were to simply hope that I'm on form and then rely on luck to come to my aid, I'd have disappeared into mediocrity years ago. Today, I know that my pre-presentation performance ritual is core to my success. It's literally the difference between gambling on my future and having the odds stacked heavily in my favour.

How do you prepare for crucial meetings? If you're like most of the professionals I work with, you make sure that you know your material backwards. You do your homework. Your slides are immaculate. You're fully prepared when it comes to content. But when it comes to emotional and performance readiness, you're under-prepared.

Only a handful of people understand the power of being Performance-Ready. They know that life is theatre with consequences. They know they have to buzz with enthusiasm. They know their colleagues and clients are going to be influenced by how they say what they say, not just what they say. They know the state they are in says more about them than any words they can say.

In November 2003, I was asked to deliver a motivational and team building session to sixty salespeople from Apotex, a leading Canadian pharmaceutical company. During the briefing session I asked the client, Dave Kohler, what kind of people I would be speaking to. Dave replied, "They are the kind of people who will give you unconditional love for the first fifteen seconds. Then they'll give you what you deserve."

Well, if it's true for Dave Kohler's team, it's true for almost everyone else. All of us are going through "time-compression," where more and more is being squeezed into less and less. If you don't connect with me first time, there may not be a second time. You've got to go from warm-up to white-hot in a heartbeat.

Whether you're nineteen or ninety, our suspension-of-judgment-time is getting shorter and shorter. It may be that God judges us only at the end of our days. Human beings judge each other on impact. What's more, once we form an impression of someone, we very rarely change it. So be impactful from the get-go. Get traction or get taken out. You have no choice. What's your pre-game preparation?

I become Performance-Ready for my seminars through a six point process that I follow religiously: Firstly, I'll ensure that I exercise before my presentation so that I'm physically energized.

Secondly, I'll listen to a fellow speaker or coach so I get my mind in flow.

Thirdly, I visualize the talk going exactly the way I want it to. I see the entire event happening just the way I want it to. I see the people getting excited. I see the standing ovation. I hear the applause. I feel the euphoria.

Fourthly, I remember a time when I performed at my Personal Best. I immerse myself in that moment. I revisit all the highlights of that experience. I make them bright and shiny in my own mind.

Then, just before I go on stage, I'll limber up my tongue and mouth with "speech-aerobics." That means saying phonetically tricky phrases rapidly. Phrases like "peter piper picked a piece of pickled pepper" or "red lorry, yellow lorry." Don't laugh and don't discount this ritual. It's common practice for actors who have to be flawlessly fluent on stage – and so do you. Nothing is more impressive than someone who hits her presentation in full fluent stride and then sustains it for the rest of the delivery.
Finally, I'll issue a command to my subconscious as follows:

> *This moment is a gift. I now command my subconscious to unleash the best in me so I can unleash the best in the people in front of me. I will use all of my power to give them an experience that will transform them forever. I am pumped. I am juiced. I am ready to give the best talk I've ever given. Yes! Yes! Yes!*

So that's my Performance-Ready Ritual. What's yours? Design one. Apply it. If it does not work for you, apply another and then another and then another. Do it. Visceral Vitality grows dramatically with conscious application.

Dr. Martin Seligman, author of *Authentic Happiness*, conjured up one of my favourite phrases, "a psychology of rising to the occasion." That's a psychology worth pursuing. That's the psychology epitomized by a Vinatieri, Rodriguez or Navratilova. Ownership of this psychology would come very close to guaranteeing that you're always on when you need to be on. Practice. Experiment. Enjoy. If you always seek to rise to the occasion, you'll never fall flat on your face.

On the other hand, if you're merely playing not-to-screw-up, you'll consistently fall short of the mark. **Success in an I've-got-no-time-I've-seen-it-all-before-now-show-me-what-you've-got environment demands**

that you bring more than you ever have before to every encounter. It helps if you've got your own formula for getting up there.

Honour your Intuition by acting on it.
Intuition: *direct perception of the truth; a keen and quick insight; pure untaught knowledge; immediate under-standing.* **(Webster's Dictionary)**

Do you have it? Are you in communion with your instincts? Do you honour your gut feeling by acting on them? Often, your intuition will tell you what to do before your head has a chance to figure it out. Right actions are revealed directly through your intuition. If you refuse to listen to it, you cannot manifest your personal power.

Intuition comes from the Latin word, *Intuare* – meaning teacher. If prayer is our way of talking to our Higher Power, then intuition is our Higher Power's way of talking to us. So listen. Trust yourself and back yourself especially when your intuition goes against the advice of others. Your Personal Best depends on it. We simply cannot be happy if we're not living in alignment with our instincts. I know that almost every regret I have comes from not heeding my inner voice.

Let me ask you this question: have you ever wanted to say something in a meeting but stayed silent because you were scared of sounding stupid? How did you feel about yourself afterwards? Worse, how did you feel when someone else said what you wanted to say and received all the kudos? If you're like me, you probably felt pretty rotten. Why? Because you let yourself down by not doing what you know you should have done.

Every time you don't do what your intuition tells you, you commit suicide by installment. You have a "mind-attack" and part of your mental muscle dies. There is a Chinese saying: "A person who bows for too long cannot stand up."

The more you talk about your intuition, the more you understand it. Have you ever felt something intuitively and then experienced an initial difficulty in describing it to others? However, if you were fortunate to be sharing it with a patient, caring person, the words eventually revealed themselves to you. Well, find as many caring and patient people as you can, and talk to them. And if you can't find any, find a pet.

There are Three Intuitive Questions that will connect you to your most valuable power-source. Ask them constantly, make them a habit and the answers will flow to you:

How do I feel about this, does it feel good?
What's the right thing to do, even if it's the hardest thing to do?
How will this action impact others – how can I benefit them?

The most effective people I know are the people who honour their intuition. There's no dead-zone separating them and their inner truth. They hear the call to action. They heed it. They do it.

Here's a national tragedy: fully one half of the population see their job as nothing more than a paycheque.

Given that we spend more than half our daylight hours at work (more like three-quarters in the winter), is it not astounding that only half of us get personal satisfaction from this activity? And if this is so, think of the huge untapped potential in the workforce that could be unleashed in the form of commitment, creativity and productivity if more employers could figure out ways to motivate their workers, or workers could figure out ways to revitalize themselves.

Here's the truth: doing something that you don't like will kill your Visceral Vitality. I can't say it any stronger than that. So, if you're currently part of the half of people who don't like their jobs, what should you do? Firstly, find something to like about your work. If you can't just leave, find a reason why it's not only bearable but also beneficial. Then, engage in a search for a new job – but make sure that you're not running away from your current challenges. Always run to something, not from something. Any which way you turn, your butt is always behind you.

What's your real age: how old do you feel?

Let me conclude this chapter by asking you one last question. It's the classic question by Satchel Paige, the baseball great who pitched until he was nearly 60: "How old would you be if you didn't know how old you were?"

In an interview with the *New York Times* (09/28/03), Van Toffler, President, MTV and MTV2, said, "I would say that my maturation process stopped at about age 19. I just said that's, like, enough. And so I work for a channel that's made the decision not to grow old with its audience, and always to be relevant and current. I mean what could fit my personality better? In order to be at this channel and succeed in this job, you have to put yourself in the mindset of an adolescent or young person who's going through major life changes."

I will be 35 years old until I'm 80. I will have that blend of youth and experience as long as I'm privileged enough to stay on the planet. By playing full out, staying curious, being perpetually fascinated and romancing everything and everyone around me, I will be my own Peter Pan. I'm 46 years old going on 36. How about you? Choose an age. Any age that's right for you. And then grow younger over time.

**LIVE IN THE
SWEET**
SPOT.

STEP 5:
Make World-Class Friends

Be Relationship Centric.
Listen With Your Third Ear.
Make Others Salivate.

5

Your "Make World-Class Friends" Self-Exploration

Here is a simple 10 point test to determine your command of this skill. For each question, rate yourself on a scale of 1-10.

- [ ] • I always look for opportunities to help others
- [ ] • I like to share my insights and resources with others
- [ ] • Most the time, I exceed the expectations of others
- [ ] • I am always courteous towards others
- [ ] • I always look for what's best in others
- [ ] • I am a great listener to others
- [ ] • I work very hard at building great relationships with others
- [ ] • I have a close personal team that makes me outstanding
- [ ] • I have a wide network of people who help me find opportunities
- [ ] • I make it a pleasure for other people to be with me

◯ **total**

- **If you scored between 85 and 100**
Congratulations. You're already a World-Class Friend.
- **If you scored between 70 and 84**
You're a good friend, now you need to become World-Class.
- **If you scored less than 70**
You've got a lot of relationship building to do.
This chapter will help you get connected.

"We are all angels with only one wing. We can only fly while embracing each other." Luciano de Crescenzo

World-Class Friend:

Someone who is there for you when you need them most; someone who enhances your perspective; a person who complements your strengths and amplifies your personal power; a mentor who shares their ideas and insights with you; an ally who builds your impact in the marketplace; a hub; an individual who helps you excel; a source of warmth and comfort; someone who gives and receives joy and excitement from you.

Relationship-Centric:

Always consciously going for the magic in others; rewarding others for the privilege of their presence; cross pollinating other people's potential; never feeling rejected; listening with your Third Ear; doing the Rapport Rumba; standing for something meaningful in the minds of our personal network; having a conscious will to do those things that we instinctively feel uncomfortable doing.

There is an ancient tale of two men talking, one from Heaven and one from Hell. The man from Hell lamented and moaned: "It is indeed a terrible place I live in. I feel an unbearable hunger all the time." The man from Heaven asked: "You mean there is no food in Hell?" The man from Hell looked at him with his drawn, emaciated face and replied: "Oh there's food, lots of it. We sit at banqueting tables heaped with the most sumptuous food your eyes could behold. But we are made to eat with spoons as long as our arms. No matter how hard we try, it is impossible to get the food into our mouths. That's the most unbearable part of Hell: I am starving in the middle of a feast."

"In Heaven," the other man began, "we, too, sit at banqueting tables laden with food. And we, too, are made to eat with spoons. Except our spoons are as long as both of our arms together. And we eat very well."

"But that's impossible," the man from Hell replied. "If we cannot feed ourselves with spoons only as long as one arm, how can you feed yourselves with spoons as long as both of your arms together?"

"Ah, but that's the point, my friend," the man from Heaven said with a smile, "we don't feed ourselves, we feed each other."

Be a World-Class Friend.

Whoever you are and whatever you are, if you're reading these words, you're human. Unlike a computer, you cannot run at 99.99 per cent effectiveness 99.99 per cent of the time. There are going to be those moments when your light goes dim. Despite your mastery of the preceding four steps to Personal Consistency, there will be times when you'll struggle to perform at Your Personal Best – even when it counts. That's the moment when you need to draw on someone else to sustain you.

I don't know about you but I'm encountering more and more of these kinds of moments. Like my friend, John Abbenda, a Private Wealth Consultant at a leading bank, I want to "eat life." And sometimes, I bite off more than I can chew. That's when I get emotional indigestion. And that's when anxiety strikes.

The greatest antidote to anxiety is the knowledge that you've got friends you can call on in the crunch moments. So no matter how threat-free your life is right now, build your Personal Defense Network. When the dark forces of Saruman come calling, you want your Aragorns, Gandalfs and Sams by your side.

David Liniger, Chairman of the Board and Co-founder of RE/MAX International, states that "a network of World-Class Friends" is the greatest asset you can have in the 2000s. Are you a World-Class Friend? And how many World-Class Friends do you have?

"Six degrees of separation" stand between you and almost any other person on the planet. According to Dave Ticoll (*Globe and Mail* 12/04/03), the science behind this pop-culture phrase dates to 1967 when Harvard psychologist Stanley Milgram asked volunteers to forward letters via acquaintances to a stockbroker whom he identified only by name, job and general location. Instead of meandering indefinitely hither and yon, a typical letter reached its destination in a mere and surprisingly manageable, six steps.

Since then, network analysis techniques, powerful computers and the Internet have turned social networking from lifestyle curiosity into a phenomenon to be harnessed for fun, results and profit. The theory contains some interesting insights. For example, **weak social ties outside a person's normal clique are disproportionately important to functions like finding a job or new information.** And though most people have few acquaintances, some special individuals called *Hubs* have many relationships.

World-Class Friends are those Hubs who are willing to invest their time, energy and relationships to help you achieve your objectives. They are the most valuable resources on earth. The more Hubs you have, the more successful you will be. My Hubs include Marta Pawych, Martin Perelmuter, Jeff Dufour, Cheryl Fairbanks, Marianne Thompson, Kevin Murdoch, Catherine Bridgman, Steve Graham, Sue Bright, Dave Kohler, Russell Bandy, Carolyn Miller, Dennis Stief and others.

So how do you build a network of World-Class Friends? It's called Habitual Generosity.

Habitual Generosity:

The free-flowing giving of time, money, energy or emotion; the constant and proactive search for ways to add value to others, especially when it's tough to do so; offering more than others think is wise; impeccable kindness and courtesy to strangers; ongoing investment in the emotional equity of others; insurance against hardship and isolation; acquiring immunity against despair; becoming the kind of person who attracts success; inviting the favours of angels.

Here's where the rubber really hits the road: how much of your time, money and energy do you give away to others?

Here's the most important question I can ask you: "Do you love helping other people?" If your answer (and only you will know) wasn't an immediate, unqualified, instinctive, enthusiastic "YES!," Your Personal Best will always be less than it can be. A passion for giving is the direct pipeline to fulfillment. The true winners are not Go-Getters; they are Go-Givers. They live by a code that demands that they always give more than they take.

It's a belief that the deepest sense of personal well-being always comes from enhancing the well-being of the people around them. The root of their generosity is the pleasure they get from adding value to other people's lives. They don't give because they're saints. They're not necessarily Good Samaritans. They give because they know that altruism really pays big dividends. They give habitually not just because it gives them pleasure to do so; they give because they know that generosity is the most lucrative investment they can make and the only true insurance against adversity.

Think about this: how many people do you know who only call you when they need something from you? Or, they're only courteous when they want something? Otherwise they don't make any effort to help, or even just lighten up your day. How do you feel about them? When you hear their voices or when you see their faces, what emotions do you experience? Resentment? Irritation? Mild annoyance? Nothing at all? The bottom line is that they have no equity with you. If you're the kind of person who is a habitual giver, you'll help them anyway, but you're in the minority.

On the other hand, how do you feel about those people who are continually there for you? Or who have gone the extra mile to help you? Or who assisted you in a really challenging moment when no one else would? If you're like most of the people who we have researched, you'll feel a powerful need to return the favour. **The truth is that people are governed by The Law of Reciprocity that states: if you do something for me, I feel obligated to return the gesture. Thus, the more you do for others, the more "currency of reciprocation" you accumulate for when you need it most.** Generosity is good business. If you develop a reputation for contribution and caring, revenue will flow back to you. The vast majority of people will repay your largesse with interest.

The recipient of your generosity is the one giving the gift of giving to you.

Go-Givers proactively search for ways to contribute to others even before they're asked to do so. Either they spontaneously offer opportunities to others when they were least expecting it, or they sense when someone needs their gift and they take action before they're asked to do so.

Let me ask you this: how many times have you known that someone needed your assistance but hadn't asked for it? How many times have you known that someone was too proud or too timid to request a favour from you? How many times have you just sensed that you could do something for someone who needed it? And how many times did you step up? If your answer is "most of the time," you're already practicing Habitual Generosity. If you're not sure, or sense that you could be doing more, now would be a good time to start.

Think about those times in your life when someone stepped up to help you when no one would give a damn. If you're like me, you can remember each and every moment with a powerful emotional surge of gratitude and affection. Maybe it was a school friend who stood up for you or stood by you when no one else would; maybe it was an employer who hired you when no one else would; maybe it was a client or colleague who believed in you when no one else would; maybe it was a spouse who saved you when no one else could; maybe it was a partner or mentor who saw in you qualities that no one else did; maybe it was the teacher who complimented you on a talent or accomplishment when no one else would. I promise you that these are the people who've made your life rich.

Now, my question to you is: how often are you playing this role in the lives of others? **Never underestimate the impact of even the smallest gesture on the well being or confidence of another human**

being. What's more, a tiny effort on your part can have a huge effect on the life of another. Make it happen.

Habitual Generosity is closely related to "extreme empathy." Extreme empathy is when we know intuitively when others need our gift, even if they don't know themselves. From the earliest age, humans develop a resistance to asking for help – especially males. How many men do you know who won't even ask for street directions? Because asking for assistance is often perceived as a sign of weakness. So, in order to engage in constant acts of generosity, not only do you have to sense when to give but also how to give. Highly gifted givers make it seem as if the recipients of their gifts are the ones who are actually doing the giving.

Go-Givers know that wealth is really the capacity to share. That's why they're happy (and wealthy).

How many people do you know who are "hoarders? These are the kind of people who are reluctant to share their resources, knowledge or ideas. They define themselves by how much they have. Their possessions, material or mental, are the source of their power. Therefore, they're constantly afraid of losing what they have. And you know what? Chances are that they will. I get so many calls from people in a state of depression because they've lost their money, house or business. The market's turned against them, a partner's turned on them, or their customers have turned away from them. The truth, though, is that they assigned the wrong meaning to their assets. They saw them as possessions to hoard or gloat over, not as resources that could empower them to empower others.

So what does wealth mean to you? What would you do if you were shown the money? For me, money means one thing: the ability to excite others. The more resources I have, the more I can influence others with my insights, and the more I can invest in media and promotion to ensure the deepest penetration of my message. And the more I can influence others, the more money I make. It's a beautiful circle. The more value I add to the people around me, the more wealth I create. But here's the important distinction: **I'm not influencing others because I'm making money; I'm making money because I'm influencing others. I know that the moment my motivation becomes purely commercial, my revenue flow will dry up.**

The Rotary Club's mission statement is perhaps the best expression of the spirit of Habitual Generosity – "Service Above Self." If you serve others, you become a giant. If you are self-serving, you shrink. Who are you serving? Who are you putting above yourself? What value are you adding to the people around you that fills you with a huge sense of purpose?

"People who are selfish have little problems but they seem big. People who are generous, have big problems but they seem little." Mother Teresa

What kind of problems do you have? How many times has someone come to you with a problem that they believe is insurmountable? However, as you look at the problem, you cannot believe how the other person can get so upset about something that appears so small. What to you is a molehill, to them is Mount Kilimanjaro.

Time and time again, I work with people who are consumed by fear and anxiety. They operate from a place of inner fear because they are only concerned about their own wellbeing. They are almost always weak. Their perennial question is: what's going to happen to me? What's in it for me? How will I cope? **Well, if you are only concerned about yourself, you will not be able to take care of yourself.** Even the smallest problems will be cause for anxiety. Almost all of your energy is focused on protecting yourself, not nurturing or feeding others. And the more your energy is turned inwards, the less able you will be to master the outside world.

If you are generous and abundant in spirit, you will handle almost anything with grace. By practicing Habitual Generosity, you open up your energy to all the people around you. They get the best part of you. You immunize yourself against fear because you are focusing on them, not on yourself. You become the kind of person other people turn to in times of difficulty. Eventually you become a leader. Not because you want to. But because other people want you. So what kind of person are you? Do people run to you or from you? Do your problems seem big or little?

I'll tell you this: I practice Habitual Generosity because the alternative is too horrible to contemplate. Twelve years ago, I became clinically depressed because I was so focused on my own problems. I made a deal with my Higher Power. We agreed that if He got me out of my mental mess, I would never take anything for granted again and I would use all my resources to help the people around me to do the same. That's why you're reading this book. It's just another installment on my lifelong contract.

Dr. Bernard Levinson, the renowned psychiatrist, states that **consistent contribution to others who need your help is the most effective non-pharmaceutical way to sustain Your Personal Best.** He advocates giving to others especially when you're down. You'll be uplifted both by the pleasure of helping someone else and the diversion of your focus from your own problems. As opposed to shopping your way back to happiness, try spending either your money or your time on someone else. You may become addicted to it. And, by the way, I'm not advocating a life of obsessive self-sacrifice here. I certainly engage in my fair share of retail therapy. I'm just suggesting an occasional change of focus. The more you do it, the more of a habit it will become. And the greater the payback you will receive.

Most of us are just hanging by our fingertips. We're running so hard and doing so much that we're stretched to the max. Emotions like security, love and recognition are in very short supply. That's why these are the three emotions we have to keep giving to others, even when we're in short supply ourselves. I'll make you this promise: neglect the emotions of the people around you, and you will perish. Generously feed the emotions of the people around you, and you will thrive.

Sustained success is not something that you chase. It's the goodwill of good people that you attract to you by the kind of person you're becoming.

Every time you practice Habitual Generosity, you become a magnet for even more goodwill. It's the great pension plan of life. You make a deposit into the wellbeing of others and life makes an even greater one on your behalf — in both your wellbeing and that of others. Every deposit yields greater and greater returns because you're fulfilling your highest responsibility — the responsibility of sharing your awesome gifts with others. As the movie says: *Pay It Forward*. Every person who you help could help someone else. Seriously, often the only difference between a cynic and an idealist is whether he's been robbed or rewarded by others.

Our challenge is to keep giving even when we've been taken advantage of. How many times have you heard someone say cynically after his generosity was abused: "That's what you get for helping somebody!" or "That's the last time I ever do anything for him again." Or "Give people an arm and they'll take a leg."

I've learnt from the hundreds of Habitual Givers who have enhanced my life that there are two kinds of recipients: nine out of ten are the kind of people who will appreciate and reciprocate your generosity, but it's the other ten per cent that will test your goodwill to the max. They are the people who take without grace or gratitude. And they are the ones who really develop your Habitual Generosity muscles. So make sure that you have at least a handful of such recipients. They are there to remind you that giving is not just about pleasing yourself; it's about assisting others for no reward.

I'm not just talking about money here. Parting with your dollars is the easy part of

Habitual Generosity. I'm talking about giving your time, effort and energy. So be nice to the person who is never nice to you; help the person who never helps anyone else; contribute to the person who never contributes to anything else. Remember, people are selfish or self-centered not because they don't want to give. They're that way for one reason: they're scared. They worry that if they give up their energy or their funds, they'll suffer. It's called a deficit-mentality – a state of mind that focuses on loss, not gain.

Something else magical happens when you engage in Habitual Generosity: you raise your mental and emotional strength. You intensify your ability to focus on the main things. You broaden your perspective. You expand your self-identity as a precious resource to the people around you, and you behave accordingly. You radiate a greater presence. You talk with a greater authority. You walk a little taller and your smile's a little broader. Possibility comes looking for you. You know why? Because you and I create our own realities by our thoughts and actions every day.

The more people sense that you genuinely want to contribute to their wellbeing, the more receptive they will be to your product or service offering. Put this concept to the test: think about the people who you enjoy working with the most. Think about the kinds of people you would like to have on your team. Aren't they all characterized by Habitual Generosity? Don't you feel as though they're willing to go further and do more for you than anyone else? The best communicators, persuaders, salespeople and leaders all come from a place of genuine generosity.

First and foremost, their mission is to make their stakeholders successful. Their going-in position is always to give the most they possibly can under the circumstances. They do it because that's the only way they know how to play. They give their all, or they don't give at all. You know why? Because people know when you're holding back. They may know it consciously or subconsciously, but they know it. And if they sense that you're not playing full out, they hold back their support or commitment. And that's the beginning of the end of the relationship.

"Create Raving Fans" Ken Blanchard

The concept of creating Raving Fans is one of my most important professional principles. So what *is* a Raving Fan?

> *A Raving Fan is your most valuable asset. She is someone who is so delighted with what you've done for her or how you've treated her that she raves about you to all her stakeholders. A Raving Fan is a walking, talking, live commercial for you and your services.*

So let me ask you: how many Raving Fans do you have? Are you delivering the kind of service that impacts people so profoundly that they feel compelled to tell others about how you made them feel? The most powerful form of advertising is simply word-of-mouth. You and I are far more likely to trust someone who we know and like than any TV, radio or press advertisement. Also, it's a whole lot cheaper.

The more you engage in Habitual Generosity, the more likely you are to create Raving Fans. Give, and you will receive the kind of kudos that leads to much, much more business. How many people do you know who give so much of themselves that they consistently create Raving Fans? If you're like most of the people I interview, you'll probably struggle to identify more than one or two.

However, here's a dual warning: firstly, when you give of yourself, make sure that what you're giving is relevant and meaningful to the recipient. Don't gush all over the other person. Don't "over-engage" her. Pitch your delivery at the right level. This takes empathy, sensitivity and experience. Secondly, don't burn yourself out or get frustrated when the other person doesn't seem to appreciate your investment in her wellbeing. That's why it's important for your generosity to be genuine and habitual. If it flows effortlessly and authentically, it will keep on flowing.

Be courteous, kind and considerate to strangers. You never know when you're entertaining an angel. And you never know who is watching.

It was 5:30 p.m. one Thursday afternoon. I was standing in line, waiting to check in for a flight from Johannesburg to Cape Town on a recent trip to South Africa. All of a sudden, I heard a collective moan from the crowd. The flight had been cancelled. Passengers were being loaded onto another plane that was only leaving at 10:30 p.m. instead of the scheduled 6:15 p.m. departure time. Passenger after passenger vented their anger on the ground hostess serving them. One after another, they complained in frustration. I watched her carefully. She never lost her poise or her cool. She demonstrated extreme grace under severe pressure.

I thought she was spectacular and when I finally reached her, I told her so. I said that my job entailed observing how people behave under stressful conditions. I told her that she inspired me because her attitude and service were world class. Well, what do you think her response was? No, I didn't get an upgrade. Instead, a little tear trickled down her cheek. She could deal with all the problems but she couldn't deal with a single genuine compliment. One kind word penetrated all the defenses impervious to wave after wave of abuse.

So why am I telling you this story? Because, although I didn't know it, standing directly behind me was the Vice President, Sales & Marketing, of one of the country's largest corporations. He saw the interaction between the ground hostess and me, as well as the emotional response I elicited. As we went through security, he told me how impressed he was with what he had just seen. He asked me what I did for a living and when I told him, he asked for my business card. Three months later, I conducted a national motivation and sales program for his corporation to the tune of $50 000.

So what's the moral of the story? Be courteous, kind and considerate to strangers. You never know who is watching. And you never know when it could be worth $50 000! Being habitually generous and genuine with your compliments pays. So when was the last time that you spontaneously complimented someone? Make sure you do it often, and make sure you do it publicly.

One last thought: use humour when expressing your aggravation to frontline service personnel – put yourself in their shoes. And watch the difference it makes to the service you receive.

"Dignity is not negotiable," says Vartan Gregorian, president of the Carnegie Foundation. There is never an excuse to vent your anger on someone else – unless they're your therapist. Whenever you shout at others, you're really manifesting your lack of emotional control. You're saying, "I'm out of control here and I can't help myself." Both of you are denigrated by the experience. So the next time you feel yourself losing control, remember these words. Remember the importance of dignity to both of you. You never know when you'll meet this person again. What you do know is that you want to have made a friend not an adversary.

Call it the "Tom Cruise Factor." According to *USA Today* (11/28/03), "He is as well-liked as any star in the industry. He is unwaveringly polite, professional and punctual: Cruise was five minutes early for his interview. When his interviewer apologized for making him wait, Cruise's reply was quick: 'Don't worry about it. Better I wait than you." So if one of the biggest names in Hollywood scrupulously practices the 3 Ps, you and I can as well.

As people become more stressed, rudeness rises. Incivility is a sure sign of fear-in-action. Irrespective of where you are and what you're going through, keep your etiquette about you while others are losing theirs. You'll make friends in all the right places because **it's in times of crisis that you make the strongest impression on the people around you. Seize every opportunity to be your best while others are at their worst. Someone important will be watching, including you.**

A person is a person because of other people. You and I are only as strong as the strength of our relationships with the people around us.

The strength of our relationships with the people around us is entirely dependent on how conscientiously we nurture those relationships. If you are not "relationship-centric," you can never thrive. You may survive, but Your Personal Best will remain way beyond your grasp.

Pam Alexander, CEO of Alexander Ogilvy Public Relations Worldwide, expresses it beautifully when she says, "Ideas will only get you so far these days. Count on relationships to carry you further. The new economy is not just about the exchange of information; it's about the exchange of relationships. With the information glut, it's tougher to know what's for real and who's for real. It comes down to trust. To build trust, invest in your relationships constantly. Help people whether or not they can return the favour. Connect them to appropriate opportunities whenever you can, even if you do not benefit here and now. By nurturing your personal relationships to help people excel, you build exponential impact in the marketplace. Ultimately their success is your success." If you want to achieve what you want to achieve, help others achieve what they want to achieve.

Quick: besides your immediate family, colleagues and very close friends, think of five people who you value very highly. Write down their names. Then write one reason next to each name why you value them so much. You have just identified five World-Class Friends.

Now, here's the crucial question: on how many lists of other's five most-valued people would *you* appear? Like any skill, some people are born connectors. They radiate charisma and warmth. They make new friends effortlessly. They are the lucky few. The rest of us have to work extremely hard at developing this vital Life Tool. Like anything else though, the more energy you invest in something, the better you become at it.

Human beings are social creatures. We crave love, acceptance and belonging. At the same time, we're terrified of being rejected or being made to feel awkward, unwelcome or small. No matter how old we are, most of us have the emotional age of a five year old. We bruise easily, so we often shy away from initiating new contacts.

In an unfamiliar setting, people would rather sit next to someone they know but do not like, than sit next to a complete stranger. Well, as the saying goes, there are no strangers – just friends we haven't met yet. Here's what I believe: **open yourself up to others and they'll respond in kind. Go for the magic**

in others and they'll find the magic in you. Walk through your fear of rejection or discomfort and you'll discover an extraordinary sense of connection on the other side.

How many times have you been in a meeting with someone where it was clear that he wasn't focused on your interests? Many people go into meetings intent on achieving their goals. The pressure is on them to deliver. So they see others as mere vehicles to help them achieve their objectives. As a result, their energy is turned inwards. Their primary consideration is self-enhancement and protection. When you're with someone like this, you can sense it immediately. A tension creeps into the encounter. Consciously or unconsciously, a resistance guides your responses to this person. Instead of letting down your guard, you put it up. The emotional distance between you increases and connectivity is minimal.

On the other hand, we've all had the pleasure of working with people who only consider themselves successful if they make us successful. They put our interests first. When they look at us, we can see their caring and commitment to us. Have you noticed that when you are with this kind of person, you feel more empowered? It's called energy feedback. It's what highly connective people give you. Are you giving it to others?

From now on, keep this World-Class Friend question in front of you at all times: how can I reward the people in front of me for the privilege of their presence? Just contemplating this question will increase your connectivity because it focuses your attention away from yourself onto the other person.

So who are the people with whom you need to connect?

What communities do you need to tap into? How can you connect with them professionally or socially? Who are the leaders and influencers in your industry? What would motivate them to want to connect with you? How can you add value to their lives? Think carefully enough and you'll discover that you know exactly what action to take. Like most of life's most lucrative payouts, the rewards accrue to people who follow through on their priorities.

What's more, the most lucrative source of new connections is really the connections you already have. In fact, think of each person in your network as a node for an entirely new network of connections. Referrals and word-of-mouth are the most effective ways to expand your network.

However, before you leverage your connections to build your personal network, make sure that you've deposited enough value into the "relationship-account." People will be motivated to assist you only if they believe you have done the same for them in the past. So, while many of us live with a bank account overdraft, none of us can afford to live with an overdrawn relationship-account, or at least not for very long.

Recently, I delivered a seminar to a group of bean growers in South Africa. I was taken on a tour of one of the bean farms. The beans are grown in long rows. At the head of each row is a beehive. I was told that the bees are needed to cross-pollinate the plants. Without the bees, there would be no beans.

Think about it: isn't that what you and I do? Aren't we all just cross-pollinators of each other's potential? How much cross-pollination are you doing? How much time do you spend consciously connecting with others, exchanging insights and ideas? It's ironic – but the less time we have to connect with others, the more we have to connect with others. World-Class Friends not only make time to connect but they maximize the impact of their connection time.

If you develop a reputation as a source of mentorship and insights, not only will people take your calls, they'll call you as well. Why don't other people return your calls? Simple, they see you as an interruption that they cannot afford. You are a waste of time. You represent just another distraction diverting them from their goals.

So dig your well before you're thirsty. Mentor, inspire, empower, energize, comfort, guide, educate, coach, and be there for others so they will be there for you when you need them most. And you will. In the heat of an emergency or urgency, finding the right resource could be the difference between breaking-through or blowing-out.

And you know what else? The person with the most reference-points wins. The person with the richest perspective sees further than anyone else. Every insight illuminates every other insight. Friends, clients, colleagues and countrymen refill our reservoirs of references.

Personal Consistency is a direct function of being able to call on the right person with the right inspiration at the right time. Are you earning the right to call others when you need them most?

Really Creative People do it in groups.

"The social ecology at many American companies says that when you're stuck, you're supposed to go back to your desk and think harder, because you were hired for your skills. At IDEO, the culture is exactly the opposite. You have a social obligation to get help." Tom Kelley, General Manager, IDEO

How often do you ask for help in the hunt for great ideas? Based on my research of hundreds of highly creative people over the past ten years, the best "Creatives" are outstanding at harnessing the energy of others to produce breakthroughs. You know how? By making the process of brainstorming or dialogue so darn enjoyable. Others want to be part of the process. They want to be stimulated. They want to be part of the excitement. They're also investing in their future brainstorming sessions by ensuring that their involvement is reciprocated.

If you want to achieve consistent creativity, you have to be a great conductor of discussion or brainstorming groups. Some people are naturally good at getting others to speak. They know how to listen, when to speak, when to lead, when to follow, how to lighten up, how to get serious, when to let the group run and when to pull it back on track.

I can promise you this: your future success will be a direct function of your ability to attract and elicit the ideas of others. The new alchemists are the people who turn the raw material of other people's opinions into marketable ideas, services and products.

So here are seven tips to facilitating turned-on brainstorming sessions, whether it's a quick one on one meeting or a formal group assembled for a specific purpose:

1. Have a very specific outcome that you want to achieve and then keep it front and centre of the group the whole time.
2. Make the session fun. Encourage people to be zany and offer extreme ideas. Walk your talk. Ensure that you project a sense of enjoyment and energy. Reward your participants for taking part in the session.
3. Be prepared and, where possible, prepare your participants with a simple e-mail or one page brief. Prepare the space for the session. Plaster the wall with paper. Have multiple triggers to get the group talking.
4. Get the other person or the group going and then get out of the way. Gently encourage everyone's involvement.
5. Ensure that you connect with a diverse range of people in the room. Most of the really great ideas will probably be generated by people who come from a very different discipline.
6. Make sure you've got technology that works, washrooms that are nearby and a constant flow of drinks, snacks and fresh air.
7. Reciprocate when other ask for your involvement. Become known as a great brainstorm session contributor. The more sessions you attend, the better you'll become.

Practise the Labrador Principle relentlessly: if you always approach people with warmth and affection, eventually your warmth and affection will be reciprocated.

Recently, I was at a friend's barbecue. It was a gorgeous, warm Sunday afternoon and there must have been at least forty people there. We were all standing and sitting around, enjoying the rays, the brewskies and each other's company. All of a sudden, Sandy appeared. He is a golden-haired Labrador who had escaped from his holding pen. He ran around excitedly, wagging his tail, obviously delighted to see so many potential purveyors of affection.

I watched as he went from person to person, nuzzling them and looking up at them expectantly with his deep brown eyes. I couldn't believe it, but despite his obvious charms, no one patted him. They were all too busy eating, drinking and talking. Instead, they just shooed him away.

Here's why I'm telling you this story: do you think this rejection worried Sandy in the least? Do you think he stopped his quest for affection because he was being ignored? Not in the least! It never occurred to him that he was being rejected. So he carried on and on, knowing somehow that love was just a chair away.

As I watched, Sandy hit the jackpot: she was gorgeous, she was tall, svelte and sexy. She loved dogs and Sandy immediately received all her affection. What's my message here? Simply this: **if you approach people with goodwill, warmth and affection, and you refuse to ever acknowledge rejection, you'll find love in all the right places.**

Let me ask you this question: do you have prospects that haven't yet responded to your approaches? Are there people who refuse to listen to you? Is there someone you want in your life who doesn't want you? Well, if there isn't, it means that either you're the most famous, powerful person on the planet or you're just not calling anyone.

Know this: the fact that people haven't yet responded to you may have nothing to do with you. It's not personal. They're not rejecting you; they're rejecting the interruption. Or they're rejecting the new insight or information because they can't yet see the value in it. Or you may be too different or too novel for them. Or they may have other priorities but would be receptive to you when the timing is right for them. Don't give up, persist like a Pit bull, do your homework, adapt yourself and your offering to what they want. Persistence overcomes resistance.

How a thick skin, a Pit Bull determination and a sense of humour won John Henning the biggest customer of his life:

John is a friend of mine who sells catering equipment to restaurants, canteens and hotels. He is remarkably successful. However, there was one customer that Henning just couldn't convert. This individual was the buyer for one of the biggest food franchisers in the Florida area. Every week, John would call him and every week the customer would tell John that he wasn't interested. John tried every sales technique he knew to get an interview with the customer – to no avail. In fact, one morning the customer became so irritated with John that he screamed at him, "@%&# OFF AND STOP BUGGING ME!!!"

Cool as a cucumber, John called the customer the following week and said to him: "I can't remember whether you told me to @%&# off or to call you to set up a meeting. I'm sure it was to set up a meeting. Am I right?" There was a moment's pause, followed by a loud peal of laughter. The ice had been broken. The customer agreed to see John. Today he is one of John's biggest accounts. What are the lessons here? Never take rejection personally. Never stop trying. Never lose your sense of humour. When you've got nothing to lose, take a risk.

The legendary Newfoundland Premier, Joey Smallwood, was once told by a voter: "I would never in a thousand years vote for you." Undeterred, he remarked to his co-canvasser, "Mark her down as 'doubtful.'"

Of course, you can push too hard, make a nuisance of yourself and not get the kind of results that John or Joey got. We all need the good judgment and sensitivity to know when to back off, before this happens.

In order to truly understand other people, we need to listen with our "Third Ear." Listen with everything you have and you will have everything.

Very rarely will people articulate exactly what they think. In fact, often they'll say the opposite of what they're thinking because they may not want to offend or confront you. World-Class Friends, therefore, listen with their "Third Ear." They listen for what is not being said. Or they listen for how things are said. Then, through their words and actions, they demonstrate their connectivity.

The biggest compliment you can pay anyone is to simply listen intently. Try it – listen to people in a way that says: "You are the only person in the world that matters to me right now. I am fully invested in your message."

In the helter-skelter work style of the new millennium, it seems we have forgotten how to listen. We all have so many priorities competing for our mind-space that we can't even hear ourselves think, never mind anyone else. The urgencies of the present coalesce with the anxieties of the tomorrow to crowd out the whispering of the Third Ear.

The Third Ear is that part of us that listens with intuitive empathy. It's the source of our truest insight and greatest connection with others. But we can only access the Third Ear if our minds are still and fully focused on the person to whom we are listening.

We are never taught to listen. I mean to really listen. We learn at the earliest possible age how to listen with only One Ear. Our parents are the models. Father, with his one eye on the newspaper and the other on the TV screen, offers one ear to his son as he talks about the baseball or soccer game he has just played. Mother says to her child: "Tell me about your day," and then continues doing the dozen chores that have to get done, stopping intermittently to answer the phone.

We learn One Ear listening well in an e-centric world. The more we have to do, the less we listen, and the more conversations we have at the same time. How many times has someone interrupted a conversation with you because his cell phone rings? How does that make you feel? How many times have you been put on hold in the middle of a conversation because the other person received a call-waiting signal? How does that make you feel? How many times has anyone asked you to repeat something because they weren't listening? How does that make you feel? How many times have you done it to someone else? How do you think they felt?

Perhaps the problem is that we are allergic to silence. We live in a massive matrix of noise. We can no longer trust or tolerate quiet. We fill all of our space with sound. Music fills the corridors. Muzak, the elevators. We have to swim through the deafening sounds of music and conversation in restaurants. Outside there is the endless drone of traffic. Even in the inner sanctum of our minds, the noise of past or future dialogue persists – "she said" – "I said" – "they did." Listening with One Ear has become a necessity of habit and conditioning. It has become a matter of survival – we have so little time, energy and mental space to spare, we have to use it sparingly.

If we persist in only One Ear listening, we are left with a sense of incompleteness, a sense of inner frustration and futility that grows stronger every day. We never truly connect with anyone else, and they never truly connect with us. It's like getting into a swimming pool only up to our thighs, feeling the welcome refreshment on a hot summer's day, and then getting out before we've immersed ourselves fully. We are constantly in the throes of a longing to give more, tell more, feel more, live more.

Listening with Three Ears is like immersing ourselves fully in the energy of the other person. It does take time but not that much more time. What it does take is a whole lot more awareness. It takes a wholehearted commitment to this moment. Not yesterday, not tomorrow, not later today. Right now, this nanosecond. Start now. If you are reading these words, be in your thoughts and emotions. If you're eating, be in the food; be in the joy and delight of all the tastes and smells. If you're drinking wine, focus on its colour, savour its bouquet, relish its finish. If you are making love, be in your fingers, in your talking, in your skin, in your loving. If you are listening to another person, be in her words, be in her world, be in her emotions. Nothing else must exist except your connection to her, your conduit to her heart and mind. Switch off everything else that can obstruct the flow.

In my seminars around the globe, I often talk to more than 500 people at a time. A large part of my program is interactive. I ask delegates questions and I need to respond appropriately. My credibility depends on how accurately I can relate to the individuals with whom I'm interacting. I must demonstrate my empathy instantly. Often, people will come up to me after the event and ask me how I seemed instinctively to understand them deeply, although I'd never met them before and I only had a few seconds to talk to them.

It's my ability to apply Third Ear Thinking in any situation that makes the instant connectivity possible. In the context of the seminar, I focus only on the person with whom I'm speaking. No one else exists in that moment. I listen to her words, her voice, her face, her eyes, her gestures, her posture, her clothes, her presence, her essence. In a heartbeat, I've immersed myself in the aura of the other person. When I respond, it comes from a place where the other person and I are no longer separated. Instead, we are humming at the same frequency. Even when I speak, I will talk in her tone and tempo, not mine. For a few moments, we become connected at the core. She feels massively listened to, validated, comforted. I feel elated, connected, alive, expanded.

My psychiatrist friend, Dr. Bernard Levinson, believes caregivers have to look their patients in the eye. Face-to-face dialogue is the only meaningful communication. "We forget how to hold our patients with our eyes. Especially if we are unable to reach forward and hold them in our arms – only the eyes are left," says Bernard. And really, that challenge is not confined to doctors or caregivers. It's the biggest challenge facing all of us as we seek to connect meaningfully with others.

Here's the secret: when you listen, give yourself. This is the hardest part. Hard, because part of the trick of giving oneself is to lose oneself, to put aside one's own importance, one's own needs for a brief time. For a moment, we have to give up our status, our world and our special place in it. Instead, we have to offer a fellow human being our space in the world – just for a few heartbeats. That's called intimacy, when we let another person into our innermost place, deep within.

Part of the reason certain professionals stay aloof from their clients or patients is their belief that this aloofness will provide them with a clear, uncontaminated objectivity so they can make cold, logical, far-reaching decisions for the patient. But this is not what the patient needs or wants. What we all want – because all of us are patients in one form or another – is to be in rapport with someone who is hearing us out, someone who is really taking in what we're saying. So be that someone for somebody else.

Ultimately, being a World-Class Friend is about Rapport, the ability to harmonise with others by demonstrating how similar you are to them. Do the "Rapport Rumba."

The primary screening question that people ask themselves before they will trust you is: "How similar is this person to me?" Think about it, have you ever said to someone: "I like you because we have big differences"? I don't think so. We connect with people with whom we think we have a lot in common. We connect with people who seem to understand us at the deepest level. In other words, we connect with people who we believe share our values.

If you really want to connect instantly with others, here's the Seven Step Lipkin Rapport Rumba. This is a simple way to bond with people instantly while laying a foundation for a meaningful longer-term relationship:

1. **Make sure that you're excited and turned-on.** If you're not connected to your personal power, you won't be able to connect with anyone else.

2. **Make sure you're rewarding the other person with what he wants or needs.** Perhaps you're simply there to entertain or comfort him. Or perhaps you're there to give him the skills to succeed. Be clear on the benefit you're there to give him.

3. **Go for the magic in the other person.** Look for the best in him. Through your words and gestures, let him know how much you value being there with him.

4. **Listen with your Third Ear.** Understand the other person's values – the forces that drive him at the deepest level. Simply ask him what's important to him in the situation at hand. Ensure that all your actions are consistent with his values.

5. **Use the actual words that the other person uses.** Listen specifically for the words he uses when he is most upbeat or excited. Every time you use these words, you will trigger upbeat emotions in his mind. Ensure that he knows you understand exactly what he wants. Then, affirm with conviction that you'll give it to him.

6. **Mirror the other person's stance and style of speaking.** Mirror his posture, tempo and tone of voice.

7. **The further the relationship progresses, the more attentive you have to be to his style, emotions and needs.**

Try the Rapport Rumba. Personalize your own steps. It must feel good for you. Let me know the results by e-mailing me on mike.lipkin@environics.ca.

Do you make others salivate?

You and I are nothing but a thought in other people's minds. So when they think of you, what do they think? Do they experience a rush of pleasure or pain? Do they instinctively smile or grimace? Do they want more of you? Or less?

What role do you play in their lives? If I were to poll ten people in your personal network, what would they tell me about you? Would they respond with pleasure and enthusiasm? Would they be able to articulate the key value you deliver to them? Would they see you as being distinctive from everybody else they know? Would they regard you as a key member of their network?

These are vital issues because human beings are Pavlovian in nature. Just like Pavlov's legendary dog, we anchor emotions to stimuli. We associate some human stimuli with pain and others with pleasure. We'll do anything to avoid painful or irritating human stimuli, but we'll do anything to connect with those people who give us pleasure or profit. **Your competence may get you into the game but it's your connectivity that wins it for you. Do you make others salivate?**

Making World-Class Friends takes guts, humanity and patience.

It takes a conscious will to do those things that you may initially feel uncomfortable doing. It takes a strong willingness to be vulnerable without becoming cynical. It also takes sensitivity. It takes just the right recipe of openness, caring and empathy. We have to customize our style for each individual in our network.

Sometimes, we'll get it right the first time and sometimes we won't. But here's the truth: you and I do not have a choice. Our relationships are where we will get our most valuable information and market intelligence. The person with the most powerful personal network wins.

So, there is no such thing as a wasted phone call, e-mail, meeting or favour. Every human interaction is either an investment or disinvestment in your future prosperity.

Often, when you least expect it, you will benefit from an investment that you may have made months, or even years, before.

"If you have only one smile in you, give it to the people you love. Don't be surly at home, then go out in the street and start grinning at total strangers." Maya Angelou

I see it all the time: people take out all their frustrations on those who have given them their love and loyalty. They invest the best part of themselves at work with their clients and colleagues. Then they come home exhausted and exasperated. They've got nothing left for their nuclear Personal Team. They shout and snap at their spouses, their children and even their pets. It's one of the saddest sights in the world: someone treating his closest family members with anger, disrespect or just plain irritation.

If there is a hell on earth, it must be a family that treats its members dishonourably. And I'm not talking about outright abuse here. I'm talking about the continual ennui, fatigue and lack of recognition that gradually extinguishes people's belief in their own personal sparkle.

In all the research we've completed, we've seen that people would rather take loneliness over being part of an unhappy family. There are very few people who would go back to an unhappy marriage, even though their standard of living may have declined by up to 50 per cent. It is simply insufferable to exist in a place where one's authenticity and dignity are constantly being denigrated.

The real tragedy is where negligence, through lack of effort and awareness, led to the break-up. I've seen men and women go into deep mourning when their spouses divorce them or their children reject them. But by then, it's too late. Something has died. **From today, make sure that the best part of you is the part you give to your family. You'll discover something amazing: you'll have so much left to give everyone else.**

I recently conducted a workshop with a multinational, billion-dollar corporation. During the program, I highlighted the need to romance and keep romancing the people closest to us. After the program, one of the delegates silently approached me. He waited for everyone else to go. Then, with tears glistening in his eyes, he told me about an event that had occurred a few days before.

He had arrived home late from work. As he was about to step into the house, his wife stopped him at the door. She told him that their five-year-old daughter was afraid to hug him. When he expressed his stunned surprise, she told him that his daughter felt rejected because he didn't reciprocate her effusive outpouring of affection. His daughter felt his distraction keenly. My words merely compounded his sense of guilt. I told him not to feel guilty because guilt is really anger turned inwards. Instead, I told him to rush home and shower his little girl with all the spontaneous love he had inside of him. I hope he did.

If one of the saddest sights in the world is someone treating his spouse with disrespect, one of the most beautiful sights in the world is long-married spouses who are totally enamored of each other. You've seen them: the way they look at each other, the tiny acts of courtesy, the subtle touches, the affectionate dialogue.

I have a colleague, who like me, is a professional nomad. He is away from home at least 100 nights a year. He has also been married for 22 years. One night, as we savoured a Johnny Walker Black 36 thousand feet above the ground on our way home from a conference, he showed me an e-mail message from his wife that he'd received just before take-off: *"Hey Boyfriend, I'm totally in love with you. I can't wait for you to get home. The lights are low and the kids are out..."* Lucky guy!

Do you have that kind of delicious thrill with your partner? Does your heart still pound at the thought of her voice, hands, touch, smell? What's happened to your interpersonal electricity? Are you seizing every opportunity to light the fire within? Do you plan evenings of passion days in advance? Or has the heat long since cooled? Do you pass each other like ships in the night? Do you speak to each other in the bored, fatigued tone, evolved out of years of apathy? How's your sex? If there is any, is it still you-make-my-heart-sing awesome? Or is it just perfunctory and automatic? Here's the truth: ultimately, your performance in the workplace is dependent on the climate in your homeplace. Sooner or later, ennui or tension at home will manifest itself at the office.

The great ones know that it requires massive energy to keep the fires burning. They make the leap from the effortless affection of the honeymoon period to the sustained, conscious loving that lasts a lifetime. Dr. Bernard Levinson, a leading sexologist, offers four simple steps to keep that loving feeling:

Have the right intent: Make sure that you truly want to excite your partner. Keep your desire at the front and centre of your mind.

Be aware of all the opportunities you have to romance your partner: Know what really turns your partner on. Know what really annoys or peeves her. There are so many spouses who really don't know what excites or extinguishes their partner's fire, even after many years of marriage. Be prepared to adapt and experiment. Let your partner know what excites you. Talk deeply and intimately about those subjects that may be taboo right now.

Prepare for intimacy just the way you prepare for a board-room meeting: Start thinking about your nocturnal delights when you wake up in the morning. Begin the ritual fifteen hours in advance by the way you look at your partner and touch her at breakfast. Call her from work. Hint at what's to come. Bring her flowers and champagne. Use the whole day to build the anticipation.

Be totally in your loving: In the moment of intimacy, be there fully. Be aware. Be imaginative. Be bold. Be uninhibited. Be adventurous. Be generous. Seek and you will find the pleasure you're really looking for.

I'm not suggesting that you ramp up your romance with your partner just to have more fun. I'm suggesting it because it will have a direct impact on your personal physical and mental health. According to the *Globe and Mail* (03/27/01), "investing time and energy in the quality of relationships means better mental and physical health for everyone involved." According to Dr. Trovato, a social epidemiologist at the University of Alberta in Edmonton, "Positive, enduring and loving relationships – free of major and prolonged conflict – are essential ingredients for healthy living."

Here's a specific warning to men: you need a woman more than a woman needs a man. Social isolation can be particularly tough on men. "Generally speaking, men tend to have fewer emotional support networks than women," says Dr. Trovato. Singlehood therefore hits men hardest, leaving them vulnerable to stress, depression, alcoholism and heart disease. So, men, love your woman as if your life depends on it – it does.

World-Class Friends stoke the fire of their relationships daily.

They're not just great lovers in their marriages or personal relationships; they manifest their passion in their relationships with every member of their inner-circle. They know that if they don't do this, their lives will slowly unravel. In all our research, we've noted that the number one reason why relationships come undone is simple neglect. It's not the "Great Betrayal" that does the damage. It's death by emotional atrophy through lack of interest or awareness.

At least half of the people we've surveyed claim that loyalty is the one of the most important attributes they look for in their current and prospective partners or colleagues. Well, the *Oxford Dictionary* defines loyalty as: *faithful in allegiance to sovereign, government or mother country.* In other words, the only entities that have the right to demand unquestioning fidelity are God, Queen and Country. Everyone else has to earn it.

Loyalty is not a birthright or permanent privilege. It's a reciprocal commitment that has to be earned daily.

It doesn't matter whether your Personal Team-member is your spouse or your salesperson, every morning you and I have to earn their loyalty anew. And by the way, this is especially true of your children. If anything, the fact that you may have sired them qualifies you for contempt rather than respect. Think about your conduct around them: are you a shining role model for the future? Or are you a walking warning?

The game starts from scratch every day. Loyalty is more perishable than the broccoli you may be having for dinner tonight. Even if you're sitting there shaking your head in disagreement, imagine what would happen if you lived your life according to this belief. You would never suffer from complacency again. And if you think that you're the beneficiary of loyalty from others, built up painstakingly over the years, prepare for some nasty surprises. In fact, right now, you may be living in denial.

A creative director at a large New York based advertising agency told me of a creative team, comprising a writer and art director that had worked for him for five and a half years. Recently, their work was becoming jaded. The creative director repeatedly tried to get them to raise their standards. To no avail. So he fired them. They were dumbfounded. They pointed out all the award-winning campaigns that they had generated for him over the years. They evidently believed that they could live on past glory – with devastating consequences.

Yesterday's achievements are like yesterday's newspaper: significant at the time but next-to-irrelevant today. It's only by consistently delivering their daily quality that we keep going back to the *New York Times* or the *Globe and Mail*. Why should people keep coming back to you?

If you do nothing else as a result of this book, I ask you to **treat even your most personal relationships as though they are 24-hour gifts that could be taken away at any time. Act each day as though you need to earn the right to have another day with the people you value most. Whatever you take for granted gets taken away.**

If your network is the radius of your influence, your Personal Team is your nucleus.

While they may be equally important, there is a huge difference between members of your Personal Network and your Personal Team. A widely developed personal network will give you the strength of weak ties. You will have a broad array of contacts that you can leverage to achieve results. You will have a rich deposit of emotional equity that you can draw on because of all the investments you have made through the years.

The members of your Personal Network occupy the perimeter of your High Performance Zone. They cannot be counted on to consistently come through for you in the crunch moments – nor do you have the right to request them to. No matter how well developed your network, if you do not have an outstanding Personal Team to help amplify and synergize your talents, you will be outperformed by someone who does.

Do you feel part of a strong Personal Team? Do you have an inner circle of people who truly "complete you"? Have you consciously and purposefully searched for and selected the best of the best to play with you? God may have given you your relatives, but you're at total liberty to choose the rest of your Personal Team-members. Choose them well because they can be the difference between a mediocre and a marvellous life.

Jack Bensimon, president of the leading Toronto advertising agency, Bensimon Byrne D'arcy, describes his agency's selection of team-members as follows: "We look for talent and decency in equal measure. Sometimes this balance is the toughest thing to achieve. Very often, we'll find an individual who is highly gifted but who just can't play nice with the other kids. Alternatively, we may find a wonderful person who has limited talent. We have to part with both of these people. They will weaken the team. We've built a great team because we've made the right choices – both during the hiring interview and after. You can't always get it right in the interview. You can sense whether someone has the right stuff but you just don't know until they're actually in the situation. If they skew one way or the other, you have to let them go. You just cannot afford to keep them on."

As I write these words, I feel an intense sense of well-being when I think of the players on my Personal Team: my wife and friend, Hilary; my partners and friends at Environics; and my agent and friend, Martin Perelmuter. Those are some of the members of my Personal Team. They are the people I need to truly thrive in the future. I know they are the best of the best, that's why I selected them. Other members of my Personal Team join and leave according to the projects I'm pursuing. A Personal Team Player can be with you for a lifetime or just lunchtime.

Each member of my personal team helps me play a different game in the league of life. Who are the members of your Personal Team? Are they world class? How do you know?

The *Oxford Dictionary* defines a team as "a set of players forming one side in a game." So if you want to win the games that you play, you'd better be on the best team. What's more, in a Free-Agent World, you're the leader of your team one day and a follower the next. This has two life-changing implications: firstly, you have to be outstanding at choosing and building great teams. Secondly, not only do you have to be an outstanding team-player, you have to be known to be a great team-player. Let me ask you this question: **Would you be the number one draft pick or the MVP of other people's Personal Teams?**

How well do you understand the nature of the multiple games that you play every day? How well have you matched your teams to those games? How well are you strengthening your teams every day? How quickly do you change your team when the game changes? Or how quickly do you take action when it becomes apparent that a team-member is not able to play the game? These may be brutal questions but they're the questions that will determine your level of sustained success.

We've all seen the consequences of not taking quick action to ensure the maximum effectiveness of the team. The longer you wait, the greater the damage and the harder it is to boot-up the performance of the team again. We simply do not have the luxury of quixotically hoping that "the situation will just sort itself out." In some cases the action may simply entail a coaching or counselling session. In others, it may entail severance from the team — either because of incompetence or lack of character.

If you're like me, I know that you've been cut from teams and that you've had to cut others from teams. It's almost always painful. However, in my experience, it has ALWAYS been for the best. Once the righteous indignation has simmered down, the smart ones regroup and move on. They know that once "the line in the sand" has been crossed, you can't go back. The fact is, there's probably an even more lucrative assignment just a couple of phone calls away.

How compelling is your vision for your teams? Do you even have a team-vision? How much energy are you investing in building a great team? Are you the human glue that binds the team? Or do you expect everyone else to serve you? Are other's Personal Teams stronger because you're on them? Here's the truth: you cannot have a strong team that consists of weak players, but you can have a weak team that consists of strong players – if they don't work extraordinarily well together.

Every company I have worked with in the past nine years has a "Corporate Vision" that is its theoretical rudder. However, even when the vision is strong, simple and compelling, it doesn't necessarily filter through the entire enterprise. That's why one of the most powerful things you can do right now is help distil your team's WHAT, WHY and

HOW (Revisit the chapter on Focus). Use the tools you've learnt so far to harness your team-members' passion to the cause.

Since the beginning of 2001, I have worked with over 300 companies in the U.S. and Canada. In most instances, I was hired to help set people on fire. In almost every situation, people ignited when we paint a picture of the future for them that resonated with their values and desires. **Paradoxically, at a time when idealism is in short supply, people want a reason to believe. In fact, the only thing stopping them from being idealistic is fear — the fear of failing, or being disappointed, or being penalized for making a mistake.**

So, for example, the driving motivation behind the Environics' partners' decision to enter into a joint venture with me in January 2001 was the vision I presented to them: "To democratize the Environics data by making them accessible to thousands of Americans and Canadians who want to thrive in the future." This book is one of the conduits through which we're translating that vision into reality.

The most important question for those people who are great Personal Team players is simply: How can I become an even better Personal Team Player?

Have you noticed that people who are really good at something want to become even better? So they keep asking the right questions and they keep receiving the right answers. Every answer then spawns a whole new range of quality questions and so the positive spiral continues.

When I entered into a joint venture with Environics, Michael Adams asked me a simple question: "*How can we help you achieve maximum success?*" A curious thing happened when he asked me this question: I focused on the answer and thought of a series of possibilities I would not previously have identified.

Try it yourself. Constantly ask your Personal Team-members how you can make them even more successful. Four things will happen: firstly, you will enhance their goodwill towards you because you are demonstrating that you are genuinely focused on their best interests. Secondly, you will help them identify *Optimal Actions*. These are the actions that lead to greatest success. Thirdly, as you and your Personal Team-members take the Optimal Actions, the entire team raises itself to another level. Fourthly, every time a team-member takes an Optimal Action, the forward momentum of the entire team accelerates.

The team develops the rhythm of success. Each Personal Team-member is encouraged, emboldened and empowered by every other team-member's achievements. The more a team wins, the more of a winning team it becomes. Starve a team of victories, and the team-psyche forgets the feeling of victory. Feed a team a steady diet of victories, small and large, and its appetite grows. What's happening to your team? How voracious is its appetite for success? And what are you personally doing to make it even bigger? Your Personal Team's wellbeing is always your responsibility.

It's one thing to be a great leader; it's an even more important thing to be a great follower.

Irrespective of who you are, you will be a leader sometimes and a follower in other situations. While you may consider yourself a good leader, are you a good follower? Do you know what your "manager, supervisor or leader" wants from you? One of the best lists of what "Your Manager Wants You To Know" was featured in *USA Today* (12/10/03). Read it and reap:

1. Don't take it personally when I'm abrupt. Bosses don't necessarily handle stress any better than anyone else does.
2. I can't make a federal case out of every issue that's important to you. When it comes to doing battle with my own boss or other departments, please let me pick my battles on your behalf.
3. I'm not King Solomon. When you and a co-worker both want the desk close to the window, play rock-paper-scissors.
4. Don't give me a reason to watch you like a hawk.
5. You're the expert on your job; not me. Don't be frustrated that I don't know the details. I have a different job description than you.
6. When you're angry with me, let me know.
7. Don't ask me to tell you what I can't talk about. Are layoffs coming? I like you but not enough to jeopardize my job.
8. Bring me problems as far in advance as possible. I can help you out of a jam if I have enough lead time.
9. Give me feedback on my management style but be tactful and constructive.
10. I can help you if you goof up, but don't anything really stupid.

Are you a FunMeister?

Are you a source of exuberance and joy to your Personal Team-members? When they think of you, do they smile with pleasure? Do your Personal Team-members really look forward to playing with you? In fact, do they truly enjoy playing with each other? Here's a Personal Team-truth: the truly great teams love being with each other. They thrive on each other's energy. They would rather play together than do almost anything else.

You and I both know when we're in the presence of great teams. There's a joy and exuberance in the players' interaction with each other. Sometimes the fun levels are loud and sometimes they're understated, depending on the culture of the team itself, but the spirit of play is always there. Think of your homeplace and your workplace: What's the FQ, the Fun Quotient, like? I guarantee you that the more fun your team is having, the better your team is doing.

So how are you fanning the Fun Quotient of your Personal Team? Is it a conscious priority for you? If it isn't, make it one. Through your words and actions, ramp up your playfulness. Surprise your team-members by what you say to them or do for them. Create events and opportunities to entertain and energize them. Put a spring in your voice and in your step – especially in winter or tough times. And, if you happen to consider yourself an introvert or a VSP, a Very Serious Person, imagine the impact your change of behaviour would have on your Team-members. It would be worth doing something mildly crazy just to see the look on their faces. Above all else, remember the cardinal Personal Team Principle:

It doesn't matter how you feel. What matters is how you make your Personal Team-members feel. By delighting them, you'll be delighted with yourself.

"Suffer fools gladly because no matter how brilliant you are, you are going to be a fool at some stage or another." Reg Lascaris

In the messy, chaotic, high-velocity future, all of us are going to make mistakes. And the better we are, the more actions we'll take. And the more actions we take, the more times we're going to screw up – which means two things:

Firstly, we have to be prepared to make a fool of ourselves over and over again. Although the image others have of us is crucial to our wellbeing, what's even more crucial is the need to do what we know we have to do when we know we have to do it. If you hold back because you're afraid of what others will think, you don't need me to tell you how you're going to feel. The wise person does immediately what the fool does eventually. Be wise.

You know what else I've discovered? People will actually admire your courage if you try something new. There are many people who want to do so many things, but they're waiting for you to do it first. The moment you take action, you make it okay for them to follow. So, right now, go and do something that you know will help you make a fool of yourself. The more you do it, the easier it gets. You may even begin to enjoy it. Others certainly will. As the legendary baseball player, Lou Brock, said, "Show me a guy who is afraid to look bad and I'll show you a guy you can beat every time."

When you do make a fool of yourself, the most appropriate strategy is to make fun of yourself in front of others before they do it. People love people who engage in self-deprecating humour. If you mock yourself, it also robs your enemies of the opportunity to do it to you. First and foremost, be a World-Class Friend to yourself – because you cannot give what you do not have.

Secondly, we have to deepen our tolerance and acceptance of all the people around us. One of the marks of individuals on the path to burnout is their impatience with people who have different views from theirs. I see it all the time. Their focus is on getting the job done with as much efficiency and speed as possible. Anyone who slows them down by offering up alternate routes is treated as a fool standing in the way of progress.

What's a fool anyway? Have you noticed that a fool is anyone who may not see things the way you do? Or a fool is anyone who makes your life challenging. Well, here's a key message of this session: the next time you find yourself arguing with a fool, make sure he isn't doing the same thing! That's part of making World-Class Friends: it's only by slowing down to listen, nurture and mentor that we can accelerate delivery of our promises. So play nice with all the people you may not think are as smart as you. They may just return the favour a few minutes later.

**LIVE IN THE
SWEET
SPOT.**

STEP 6: Learn And Let Go

6

Adopt a Beginner's Mind. Get Better. Travel Light.

Your "Learn and Let Go"
Self-Exploration

Here is a simple 10 point test to determine your command of this skill. For each question, rate yourself on a scale of 1-10.

- [ ] • I'm fascinated by life: it always amazes me
- [ ] • I'm a curious person: I want to know more about everything
- [ ] • I'm always looking for better ways to do something
- [ ] • I forgive other people easily
- [ ] • I'm great at asking positive questions
- [ ] • I consciously learn from my mistakes and setbacks
- [ ] • I have great mentors and coaches around me
- [ ] • Other people see me as a great mentor or coach
- [ ] • I interact with a wide diversity of different people
- [ ] • I am very open to other people's points of view

◯ total

- **If you scored between 85 and 100**
Congratulations. You're a True Student.
- **If you scored between 70 and 84**
You're learning but you can absorb so much more.
- **If you scored less than 70**
You're missing out on all the inspiration around you.
This chapter will help get you plugged in.

"When the Student is ready, the teacher will appear."
The Talmud

A Westerner wishing to study Buddhism is interviewed by a priest preparatory to beginning the journey of Buddhist thought. They have tea. The Priest pours. The tea fills the cup. He goes on pouring. It overflows. The tea gradually fills the saucer. Again it overflows and begins to lake and seep across the table. The intending student is alarmed. Finally, in agitation, he calls out, "Please stop. The cup is full."

"You are like this cup," the priest responds, "I can't fill you. Everything I give you will flow over the top. I have to empty you first . . ."

That's what Learning and Letting Go really means: adopting what the Buddhists call a *Beginner's Mind*. **There is one Platinum Thread that runs through all my research with the most successful people I've met: they never lose their Beginner's Mind. No matter how much they've achieved, they are massively receptive to new insights and ideas. That's what keeps them fresh and invigorated.** Their Beginner's Mind protects them from stagnation and boredom. They open themselves up to life and life opens itself up to them.

You know you're in the presence of these Master Learners by their attention to the people around them. You observe their sense of wonder. You feel their desire to grow. You perceive their lack of bias. You hear their questions. You resonate with their interest in you.

Here's what I've discovered: you cannot stay On-Fire unless you're continually refueling your knowledge and imagination. Performing at Your Personal Best requires a perpetual fascination with the lessons of life.

Sometimes these lessons are pleasurable: conversations with remarkable people; reading illuminating books; surfing with Google; acquiring a new skill; travels to distant places; being coached by a skilled and caring mentor; participating in vibrant programs; winning an important deal or beating a key competitor.

Sometimes these lessons are painful. They're called setbacks, mistakes, oversights, upsets, losses, and defeats (SMOULD). People-On-Fire get better with every SMOULD. Others get bitter. And that's the difference between being On-Fire and being extinguished. Fascination is bright. It's flammable. Bitterness is heavy. It's hard. It's already burned up.

The Godfather of consistency and fascination is Larry King. By his own estimation, King has conducted roughly 45,000 interviews over his 46 years in the business. Here's how he describes it: "It's incessant with me. Who, what, where, when, why, never leaves me. I'm just insatiably curious, which helps in my job. I'm the kind of person you don't want to sit next to on an airplane – I'll drive you nuts." How about you? What's your CQ – Curiosity Quotient? How enthralled are you by the people around you?

Martina Navratilova, who won her 20th Wimbledon title (mixed doubles) at the age of 46, provides an inspirational metaphor for life when she wrote in the June 2003 issue of *Tennis Magazine*: "You should approach Tennis as a game of constant education. Remember that nobody grows old merely by living a number of years. They grow old when they abandon their enthusiasm to learn."

Let go and move on.

People-On-Fire understand that pain is often a more powerful motivator than pleasure. Think about it, when have you grown the most? When have you learnt the most? Which people have helped you grow and learn the most?

It's during your toughest moments that your most valuable education occurs – even though it may not feel like it at the time. The need to avoid pain is far stronger than the need for pleasure. **The challenge is to extract an empowering learning from the experience, not one that inhibits your future performance.**

Once upon a time, two monks were on their way back to their monastery when they came to a strongly flowing river, which they would have to cross. Both were big, powerful men, so crossing the river did not pose a problem. As they were about to cross, however, they noticed a frail young girl standing about fifty yards downstream from them on the same side of the river. She looked worried because she knew she could not cross the river by herself, and night was falling fast.

The first monk looked at the girl and decided that he couldn't help her because of his vow of celibacy, which forbade him even to touch a woman. The second monk looked at the young woman and was concerned about her safety. He knew that, if he didn't help her, she would have to spend the night by the river until she could cross it when it subsided in the morning. He balanced his vows of celibacy against the well-being of a fellow human being. He knew that if he didn't help her and something terrible happened to her, he would never be able to forgive himself.

He called to the young woman, put her on his shoulders and carried her across the river. The moment he reached the other side, he put her down and bade her farewell.

Then he continued on his way. Five hours later, as the moon rose high in the sky, the first monk said to his companion: "You should be ashamed of yourself. You violated your vows of celibacy by carrying that girl across the river." The second monk replied calmly: "Yes, but I let go of her five hours ago. You're still carrying her around."

I meet too many people who are carrying too heavy a load. Their past SMOULD has become their burden. They're traveling heavy. Their baggage is preventing them from moving at the speed of the new normal. Their mental arteries are clogged. They lurch from one anxiety attack to another. All because they curse the very things that are their blessings. You cannot re-live the past, but you can re-view it.

Revisit those experiences that haunt or hassle you. Think of those people who've "done you wrong." Seriously, write down at least three MEEs – Momentous Emotional Events – or SDPs – Significantly Disturbing People. These are the crucial experiences or negative people that have materially influenced your thinking and your behaviour. Next to each MEE or SDP, write down the most valuable lessons they've provided you.

Here are my three MEEs/SDPs: the death of my father at the age of 43 when I was 17; an episode of clinical depression when I was 31-years-old; and a business associate who betrayed my trust when I came back to Canada in 2001 at the age of 43.

All three events have made the greatest contribution to my current level of happiness and expertise.

My father's early demise has made me grateful for every day and fiercely committed to physical fitness.

My episode of clinical depression has given me both a deep empathy with others and an understanding of human suffering. It is directly responsible for leading me towards a career as a professional speaker specializing in motivation and personal excellence. Every hour, it serves me as a constant command to walk my own talk so I never go back there again.

The business associate who betrayed my trust taught me to listen to my own instincts. He taught me how to negotiate. He taught me how to compartmentalize my emotions so I could continue motivating my clients even when I was engaging him in legal combat. He taught me how strong I really could be. Most importantly, he led me to a whole new range of professionals who share my values and forward-vision.

So wear your scars proudly. A scar is the site of a wound that has healed. It's a badge of achievement and courage. There is no one around you who isn't carrying one. It's just

that some may not be visible. Take strength from them. Don't be afraid to show them off. They may just help you heal others as well.

Whatever you're going through in your life right now is what you're meant to be going through in your life right now because that's what you're going through in your life right now.

Read that line again. It's the difference between people who embrace their realities and those who run from them. It's the difference between learning and losing. Whatever has happened was meant to happen because it happened. And it happened to grace you with learning so you can become the most that you can be.

As Einstein said, "God does not play dice with the universe." The moment you accept the rightness of your past and present, you can begin to craft the right future. Hold on to your mistake only for as long as it takes to extract the learning from it, then let it go. **A mistake is like a ripe, juicy fruit. If you enjoy at its best moment, it's immensely satisfying and nutritious. If you keep it too long, it rots.**

I'll tell you this: there is not a Person-On-Fire I've researched who doesn't still blame themselves for mistakes they've made. Despite their best intentions, they still look back in anger at themselves. Despite everything I've written in this book, there are a handful of things I've said and done that I don't think I'll ever be able to truly let go of. The sharp burst of pain I feel when I think of them will never be blunted. I've learnt to live with it. The pain is the reason why I'll never make the same mistakes again.

Think about this: what's the message you're being sent by your brain when you feel pain (of the non-physical kind)? Something is wrong. Something needs to be stopped or changed. Something needs to be fixed.

So don't make the pain a source of pain. Listen to its message. Interpret it in a way that empowers you and Move On. **Staying On-Fire means living according your highest standards while living with your biggest screw-ups.** There's a fine balance between the two. If you don't live according to your highest standards, you cannot achieve Your Personal Best. But if you beat yourself up when you fall short of them, you'll blow out. Here's my message: Forgive yourself for whatever has happened in the past. You have to. If you don't make peace with what has happened, you'll be at war with yourself. And then, it's over.

And by the way, what's the message that your brain sends you when you feel fear? Maybe it's: RUN AWAY. But I believe it's simply that something is about to happen and you'd better be prepared. Fear is saying: get ready. Do what has to be done to rise to the challenge. Unleash your Inner Thunderbolt.

The Lessons of the Princess and The Ogre

Once upon a time, there was a young princess who had just completed her military studies under a world-renowned teacher. Her reward for successfully completing his studies was the gift of five weapons from the school. Henceforth, she would be known as Princess Five-Weapons. Armed with her newly acquired knowledge and weapons, she set out on the road leading to the city of her father, the king. On the way, she came to a village at the entrance to a large forest. The people of the village warned her not to enter the forest. They pleaded with the Princess,

"Princess, do not enter the forest. An ogre named Sticky Hair lives there. He kills every man he sees."

But the princess was confident and fearless as a lioness. She entered the forest. When she reached the heart of the forest, the ogre showed himself. He was as tall as a palm tree. His head was as big as a house. He had the beak of a hawk. His eyes were black and bloodshot. His hair was as long and slithery as a thousand pythons. His belly was covered with blotches. His hands and feet were dark green. He gave off a rotting stench.

"Where are you going?" the ogre demanded.

"Halt!" shouted Princess Five-Weapons with great confidence, "You are my prey, Ogre, be careful about attacking me. I have arrows steeped in poison. I will kill you where you stand."

Having thus threatened the ogre, the young princess fitted an arrow to her bow and let fly. The arrow stuck to the ogre's hair. The princess shot another twenty arrows at the ogre. All stuck to the ogre's hair. The ogre shook his head and all the arrows fell to the ground. He advanced towards the princess. But the princess was not afraid. She threatened the ogre a second time and drawing her sword, she delivered a masterly blow. Once again, the sword stuck to the ogre's hair. Then the princess smote the ogre with a spear. That also stuck to the ogre's hair. Then she smote him with a club. That also stuck right to his hair. Then she struck him with her hatchet. It too stuck to the ogre's hair. When the Princess saw that all her weapons had stuck to the ogre's hair, she shouted,

"Master Ogre, you have never heard of me before. I am Princess Five-Weapons.

When I entered this forest infested by you, I did not rely on my weapons to slay you. I relied only on myself. Now I am going to beat you and pound you into powder and dust."

Having thus made known her intention, she struck the ogre with her right fist. It stuck to the ogre's hair. She struck the ogre with her left fist. That also stuck. She kicked the ogre with her right foot. It stuck to the ogre's hair. She kicked the ogre with her left foot. That also stuck to the ogre's hair. Then Princess Five-Weapons said to the ogre,

"I will beat you with my head and pound you into powder and dust."

She beat the ogre with her head. That also stuck right to the ogre's hair. Princess Five-Weapons, stuck five times in the ogre's hair, dangled from the ogre's body. But for all that she was unafraid, she was undaunted. As for the ogre, he thought:

"This is some lioness of a woman, some woman of noble birth. No mere woman. For although she has been caught by an ogre like me, she appears neither to tremble nor to quake. Of all the humans I have met and eaten, I have never, never known a woman like this one. Why is this woman not afraid?"

Not daring to eat the princess, he asked,

"Youth, why are you not afraid? Why are you not terrified of death?"

"Ogre, why should I be afraid? For in one life, one death is absolutely certain. What's more, I have in my belly a thunderbolt for a weapon. If you eat me, you will not be able to digest that weapon. It will tear your insides to tatters and fragments. It will kill you. If you eat me, we'll both perish. That's why I am not afraid."

"What this youth says is surely true," thought the ogre, terrified by the thought of death. "From the body of this lioness of a woman, my body would not be able to digest even a fragment of flesh as small as a kidney bean. I'll let her go."

And he let the Princess go. The princess then admonished the ogre. She warned him never again to eat humans. She transformed him into a spirit entitled to receive offerings in the forest. Then she went back to the village, told the people that the ogre no longer presented a threat and went on her way.

The tale of Princess Five-Weapons was adapted from a myth related by Joseph Campbell in his audio-program, *The Hero With a Thousand Faces*. Campbell, in turn, adapted it from Eugene Watson-Burlingain's *Buddhist Parables*. I love this tale because it embraces the universal conflict between fear and courage, life and death, the known and the unknown, trusting oneself versus going with the crowd, David versus Goliath.

The princess in the story could only prevail because of the "Thunderbolt" she knew she possessed within her. This Thunderbolt transcended her five senses. Her five "weapons" were of no use against the ogre. All the training and skills she had acquired couldn't prepare her for the unknown danger of the ogre. It was the princess's innate confidence and courage that empowered her to outmaneuver the ogre. When all her external resources failed her, the princess went within. She never hesitated. She was not burdened by past defeats or bogeymen. At no point did she ever doubt that she would not only survive, but that she would subdue the ogre.

There is another reason why I love this story. **Often, we only realize and use our power in the most extreme circumstances.** Every day, we read about deeds of heroism performed by people who were pushed to the very edge. Until that fateful moment when they are forced to fly or die, these people may have let their power lie dormant within them. It took a colossal, life or death event for them to manifest their power.

The Five Learning Questions

From Five Weapons to The Five Learning Questions. These are the five questions that need to be tattooed onto your consciousness so they become instinctive. The New Reality means that every day, you and I will be faced with a new Ogre who needs to be transformed. Here are the Five Questions that will help you unleash your inner Thunderbolt:

Learning Question One: **What's great about this?**
Learning Question Two: **What am I focusing on in this situation?**
Learning Question Three: **What am I learning here?**
Learning Question Four: **What will I do differently in the future?**
Learning Question Five: **Why am I grateful for what just happened?**

These Five Questions made this entire book possible. In fact, they made my other two best-selling books possible as well. In 2001, when I completed my first book, *Your Personal Best*, after having just arrived back in Canada, I offered it to a number of publishers. The feedback I received was all the same: Thank you but no thank you. So I asked myself the Five Questions:

What's great about this? At first I thought: NOTHING! Then I thought about how I was at least walking my own talk. I was in the game. I was celebrating the struggle. I was trying my absolute best to establish myself. I was out there, banging the drums, letting everyone know how awesome my book was. I was taking action, not taking no for an answer. I was developing my stamina and my resourcefulness.

What am I focusing on in this situation? At first, I was focusing on how ignorant all these publishers were. I focused on my frustration. Then, I focused on my need to break through. I focused on finding a solution. I knew my books were the cornerstone of my career and my company. My books comprise my material for my sessions. They also lend me the credibility that persuades clients to hire me. No books: no livelihood. Failure was not an option.

What am I learning here? I was learning how my new marketplace worked. I was learning about the "old way" and the "new way." I learnt that publishing my book through a traditional publisher was the old way. It would take almost two years. I would make hardly any money. And by the time it was published, many of the facts would be obsolete. I learnt about the "new way": digital publishing – how to store your material online and print to order so that cash was not tied up in inventory. I learnt who could help me design, edit and market my book. I learnt that publishing could become a major part of my business. In fact, since *Your Personal Best* was published at the end of 2001, I have sold over $1 million worth of books and CDs.

What will I do differently in the future? I will only publish my work through Environics/Lipkin. I will constantly adapt my material to resonate with a rapidly evolving marketplace. I will explore ways of publishing my work online. I will find ways to translate my work into new audio and video programs as well as public seminars. I will collaborate with other talented people do help them do the same. I will find new allies and resources that will help me enhance my acuity and impact.

Why am I grateful for what just happened? I would never have developed a thriving business if a publisher had accepted my manuscript. I would never have developed all the skills entailed in bring a book to market. I would never have experienced the exhilaration of meeting so many outstanding professionals along the publishing value chain. I would never have made such a high ROE - Return on Energy.

Once upon a time, in a desert land far away, there lived a humble man called Ahmed. Ahmed didn't have much, but what he did have were two assets that served him well: a marvellously calm temperament and a magnificent black stallion. The stallion was not only Ahmed's pride and joy; it was also his means of making a living. For a handsome fee, neighbours from miles around would bring their mares to Ahmed to be "covered" by his stallion. Every time one of these neighbours laid eyes on Ahmed's stallion, they would sigh with envy. "You are so lucky to have this horse," they would say to him over and over again. "Maybe and maybe not," Ahmed would reply enigmatically.

Then, one day, tragedy struck. The stallion's caretaker left the stable door open and the horse disappeared. The neighbours heard of the tragedy and called Ahmed with their condolences. "This is terrible news," they said to him. "Maybe and maybe not," he replied enigmatically.

Three days later, the horse reappeared as if by magic. What's more, he brought with him two other stallions that he had befriended while wandering in the desert. The neighbours called to congratulate him. "Now you've got three stallions to hire out. You're going to be rich. You're so lucky. This is wonderful news," they cried. "Maybe and maybe not," Ahmed replied enigmatically.

Now, Ahmed had a sixteen-year-old son, Rachbar, whom he loved very much. Rachbar loved horses and he was a natural horseman. He saw the new stallions and immediately mounted one of them. The wild horse felt the strange, unwelcome weight on his back and threw the boy off. As Rachbar landed, he broke both legs. When the neighbours heard the news, they immediately called Ahmed to commiserate with him. "We are so sorry for you and your son," they cried, "This is terrible news." Of course, Ahmed replied enigmatically, as he always did: "Maybe and maybe not."

The next week, it was announced that an adjacent state had declared war on Ahmed's country. The government, desperate for troops, conscripted all boys over the age of fifteen for battle. These boys had little or no military training. Their chances of survival were slim indeed. But the government couldn't take Ahmed's son because his legs were broken. So when the government took all the neighbours' sons for battle, they looked enviously at Ahmed and cried in unison: "You're so lucky!" And what was Ahmed's response? You guessed it.

What Ahmed knew, and what most of us have still to discover, is that **there is a natural equilibrium and harmony in all things. What seems like a massive loss today will help us succeed tomorrow.** Let me ask you this question: how many times have you experienced a loss or defeat that you believed was a personal tragedy? How many times have you allowed this loss or defeat to weigh you down or hold you back? And, then, how many times has this loss or defeat turned out to be of massive benefit to you? In fact, how many times have you actually been grateful to the initial mishap or apparent misfortune because of what transpired afterwards? Almost all of the time, right?

Welcome to The Equilibrium Paradox — the epicentre of Your Personal Best

Salman Rushdie, in his book, *Midnight's Children*, expressed the essence of The Equilibrium Paradox when he wrote: "All games have morals. And the game of Snakes and Ladders captures, as no other activity can hope to do, the eternal truth that for every ladder you climb, a snake is waiting just around the corner. And for every snake, a ladder will compensate. Implicit in the game is the unchanging two-ness of things, the duality of up against down, of good against evil."

Quite simply, the quality of your future is directly related to your mastery of The Equilibrium Paradox. Mastering The Equilibrium Paradox means never becoming frustrated again because it means understanding that there is no such thing as a false step. There is no such thing as "spinning wheels" or "cooling your heels" or "letting the grass grow under your feet." Every experience, no matter how minute or monumental, is a potential deposit in Your Personal Best Account if it's evaluated in the context of The Equilibrium Paradox.

Like Goethe, people who understand and leverage The Equilibrium Paradox know that "mountains cannot be surmounted except by winding paths." They know that life is full of twists and turns. **Sometimes you may even have to move away from your goal to move towards it. Sometimes, you may have to keep moving forward even when you can't see where the path is leading.** Sometimes, you may have to live for a prolonged period in the darkness in order to fully appreciate the light. Two things, though, must remain absolutely constant: your desire to be Your Personal Best and your faith in your ability to get there. I meet so many people who have become permanently tired or cynical. They've joined the ranks of the "Walking Wounded." They are surviving, but they've lost their passion and drive.

Bryce Courtenay, in his novel, *The Power of One*, states, "Life is about losing things." It's true. Think about it: every passage of our lives is marked by the loss of something that we believed was indispensable at the time — a person, an emotion, a position, a possession or a principle. And, yet, after each loss we emerged stronger than before, provided we leveraged *The Equilibrium Paradox*. If we didn't, we sank into the mire of anger, self-pity and depression.

After talking to over a million people in twenty-two countries, I've discovered that only a small minority of people understand the essence of The Equilibrium Paradox: **Life defies fairness or logic but it always rewards those who embrace it unconditionally.** As Viktor Frankl wrote in his classic work,

Man's Search For Meaning: "It doesn't matter what you expect from life. What matters is what life expects from you." It's not your conditions; it's your decisions about your conditions that determine whether you consistently play at Your Personal Best.

One of the greatest stories of responding to life's expectations by forgiving and letting go is the story of Graham Snyder, father of the late Atlanta Thrashers hockey player, Dan Snyder. Dan was killed in a car crash where the driver was his teammate, Dany Heatley. It's estimated that Heatley was driving his Ferrari at 80 miles an hour around a curve when it slammed into a brick pillar, ripping itself in half.

As reported in the *New York Times* (10/19/03), Graham Snyder embraced Dany Heatley at his son's funeral. "It felt like the right thing to do," Graham said. "This is what came naturally. We felt it was the best thing for a young man like Dany, but it was also the best thing for us, too. If we were to hang on to bitterness or anger, that wouldn't help us heal, either."

Whatever the root of the Snyder's family's compassion, their response to the loss of their son may save the rest of Heatley's life – emotionally and competitively. What's ahead of Heatley could have been much darker if not for the support Graham and his wife, LuAnn, displayed in the hospital after the crash. Even before their son died, while he was in a coma, laying in the hospital, the Snyders would ask, "How is Dany doing?"

Amazing how expandable a heart can be. The Snyders have reached beyond the boundaries of their loss to help save the rest of Heatley's life. "For Dany to carry on, he will need a lot of help," Graham said. "I think it would be a far greater tragedy if two lives were lost over this."

If Graham and LuAnn Snyder can manifest this kind of magnanimity, what leaps of faith and forgiveness can you make?

If you're a Geezer or a Boomer, find a Millennial or an Xer to mentor you.

There's a one out of two chance that you're one of the fifty percent of Americans or Canadians who are over forty years old. That means you're a Geezer (58+) or a Boomer (40-58). It also means that you may be out of touch with emerging trends, technology and mega-opportunities.

My advice? Find a reverse mentor who is an Xer (23-39) or Millennial (22-). Find someone to tell you what's really going on. Ask them what they think. Then really, really listen. Suspend your judgment and you may just hear a solution or an opportunity. To quote the Wall Street Journal (11/11/03), "Workplace technology has changed radically in the past decade and the boom of the late 1990s propelled many younger people into more senior positions faster, helping to break down traditional hierarchies. The rate of change has accelerated so much that people's experience of work is just different."

The *Wall Street Journal* offers four simple tips for reverse mentoring:
    Make mentoring a two-way street.
    Set objectives: have a schedule of times to meet and pursue a list of goals.
    Treat each other with respect
    Consider generational differences

Remember, **experience can be the ultimate liability if it's out of touch with the here-and-now.** Millennials and Xers are not labouring under the disadvantage of past paradigms. While their ideas may not have stood the test of time, they are emblematic of the times. So make the time to keep up with the times. And if you've got Millennial or Xer kids, spend more time with them. Talk to their friends. For the price of a couple of beers, they'll teach you what you never knew you didn't know.

The six most important words in the English language: I admit I made a mistake. Say them and save yourself time, money and the goodwill of others.

Have you noticed how few people are willing to admit their mistakes? Have you noticed how much fewer are willing to admit their mistakes immediately? Have you noticed what happens to your view of the other person the moment they admit their mistakes? How about you? Do you admit your mistakes and move on? Do you admit your mistakes to other people, tell them how you're going to correct them and then follow through

If you want to diffuse the anger or resentment of others towards you, admit your mistakes quickly. Often, all it takes to foster forgiveness is the willingness to assume responsibility for the mistake. Sometimes it even pays to take responsibility when the fault isn't clearly yours. If you're the person with the lightest ego and the thickest hide, you're the person who can help everyone move forward.

Admitting your mistakes will also save you a lot of money. Financial analysts agree that reluctance to admit mistakes is the major reason why investors find it so difficult to sell their non-performing stocks. According to the *Globe and Mail* (03/27/04), people's reluctance to part with an underperformer will emerge again and again.

Practice saying these six words as often as you can: I admit I made a mistake. Follow it with another six words: I take

responsibility for my actions. Then follow it with these six words: Here is how I'll fix it.

Be a Cultural Mongrel. There are no borders anymore. Borrow from everyone. Integrate the best to achieve Your Personal Best.

The world is home to some six billion people who reside in the cities and countryside of about 200 nations. To grasp the "social shape" of the world, imagine for a moment the planet's population was reduced to a single settlement of 1000 people. A visit to this "global village" would reveal that more than half (575) of the inhabitants are Asians, including 200 citizens of The People's Republic of China. Next in terms of numbers, we would find 130 Africans, 125 Europeans and about 100 Latin Americans. North Americans – including people from the United States, Canada and Mexico – would account for a mere 65 village residents out of 1000.

So doesn't it make sense, wherever in the village you happen to live, that you should know something about your neighbours? Because if you don't, at some point you are going to be taken by surprise.

As someone who has worked in Australia, Canada, America, South Africa, Dubai, Britain, Spain, Egypt, China, India, Nigeria, Ghana, Kenya and Japan over the past few years, I now feel as if I belong anywhere; and that's why I now feel so comfortable in multicultural Toronto. It's not that cultures, like technology, are converging. My friends in New Delhi are wildly different from my friends in Toronto. The social and business etiquette in Sydney Australia is dramatically divergent from that of the Sinai in Egypt. But it is the very differences among cultures that give me a sense of belonging to the globe, not to a nation.

I learnt a long time ago that my way is not the only way. In fact, it's not even the best way. I learnt that people who disagree with me are probably right as well. I learnt that the quickest way to get from here to my Personal Best may be around the world. And I've learnt that being correct by doing exactly the right thing is not what's important, being continually fascinated is.

I'm an economic, social and psychological nomad. Born in the UK, raised in South Africa, I immigrated to Canada, and I work wherever a client needs insights on motivation, persuasion and adaptation. I have dual citizenship and even my accent is a hybrid of British, South African and North American. I play multiple roles and I am the proud owner of multiple identities. What I know for sure, though, is that my expertise as an enabler of others is due primarily to my kaleidoscopic exposure to humanity. I have learnt about humility in India, warmth in Ghana, partnership in Dubai, energy in America, courtesy in Canada, resilience in Zimbabwe, re-invention in Uganda, happiness in Mauritius and forgiveness in South Africa.

Evolutionists will tell you that early man, the hunter-gatherer, would have to traverse large expanses during a hunt or to forage. He would have to recognize landmarks and patterns in the terrain both in order to track his prey and to find his way home afterwards. His ability to process information at great distances gave him a huge advantage over his predators and rivals, who had to rely on their sense of smell, thus greatly restricting their domains. His travels expanded his "cognitive maps" and "knowledge structures." And when he returned home, he transferred his broadened mental horizon and physical skills to his Personal Team.

So what's changed in the past few million years? Zero. **Those who explore, learn. They absorb the lessons of multiple contexts. The differences they encounter on their journeys empower them to recognize differences in their own backyard. They have a massive edge over their more sedentary, less mobile compatriots.**

Learning is the acquisition of knowledge, skill and ability from new experiences. It's the collaboration between the individual and his environment. The more situations an individual goes through, the more the individual learns – especially if the situations are intense. Those experiences may entail interaction with others, or they may involve a deeply private epiphany. But they are all accelerated and intensified through encounters with other cultures, countries and, of course, cuisine.

So are you one of the new Cultural Mongrels? Are you a composite of different experiences, influences and nationalities? There are no more national domains. There are just separate neighbourhoods in the rapidly converging community called Planet Earth. What happens in the neighbourhoods called India, Ireland or Indonesia has a massive, almost immediate impact on the neighbourhoods of Argentina, Australia and America. There is no such thing as a superior national culture; only superior individuals who have embraced the global challenge of opportunity.

Here's a final warning: if you disengage, you atrophy. Whatever you don't use, you lose. If you're only concerned about protecting yourself, you will be defenceless. You'll drown in your own moat. Your perspective will be warped because it lacks the reference points provided by others beyond your immediate circle.

If you go against the flow, eventually the current has to win. From the Internet to Immigration to Investing to Innovation, the barriers are tumbling. **The world is a porous planet. Osmosis ensures that everything permeates everything else – including your life.**

A Buddhist Priest; Travelling Monks; A Sticky-haired Ogre; An Arabian Horse Breeder; Cultural Mongrels. You must admit: I've rolled out a cast of exotic teachers to help you learn and let go. I want to finish with one of my all-time favourites – lessons in teamwork from an age-old fable:

The Tortoise And The Hare

1. Once upon a time a tortoise and a hare had an argument about who was faster. They decided to settle the argument with a race. They agreed on a route and started off the race. The hare shot ahead and ran briskly for some time.

   Then seeing that he was far ahead of the tortoise, he thought he'd sit under a tree for some time and relax before continuing the race. He sat under the tree and soon fell asleep. The tortoise plodding on overtook him and soon finished the race, emerging as the undisputed champ. The hare woke up and realized that he'd lost the race.

The moral of the story is that slow and steady wins the race.
This is the version of the story that we've all grown up with. But then recently, someone told me a more interesting version of this story. It continues.

2. The hare was disappointed at losing the race and he did some soul-searching. He realized that he'd lost the race only because he had been overconfident, careless and lax. If he had not taken things for granted, there's no way the tortoise could have beaten him. So he challenged the tortoise to another race. The tortoise agreed.

   This time, the hare went all out and ran without stopping from start to finish. He won by several miles.

The moral of the story? **Fast and consistent will always beat the slow and steady.**

If you have two people in your organization, one slow, methodical and reliable, and the other fast and still reliable at what he does, the fast and reliable chap will consistently climb the organizational ladder faster than the slow, methodical chap.

It's good to be slow and steady; but it's better to be fast and reliable. But the story doesn't end here.

3. The tortoise did some thinking this time, and realized that there's no way he can beat the hare in a race the way it was currently formatted. He thought for a while, and then challenged the hare to another race, but on a slightly different route.

   The hare agreed. They started off. In keeping with his self-made commitment to be consistently fast, the hare took off and ran at top speed until he came to a broad river. The finishing line was a couple of kilometres on the other side of the river. The hare sat there wondering what to do. In the meantime the tortoise trundled along, got into the river, swam to the opposite bank, continued walking and finished the race.

The moral of the story? **First identify your core competency and then change the playing field to suit your core competency.**

In an organization, if you are a good speaker, make sure you create opportunities to give presentations that enable the senior management to notice you. If your strength is analysis, make sure you do some sort of research, make a report and send it upstairs. Working to your strengths will not only get you noticed, but will also create opportunities for growth and advancement.

The story still hasn't ended.

4. The hare and the tortoise, by this time, had become pretty good friends and they did some thinking together. Both realized that the last race could have been run much better. So they decided to do the last race again, but to run as a team this time.

   They started off, and this time the hare carried the tortoise till the riverbank. There, the tortoise took over and swam across with the hare on his back. On the opposite bank, the hare again carried the tortoise and they reached the finishing line together. They both felt a greater sense of satisfaction than they'd felt earlier.

The moral of the story? **It's good to be individually brilliant and to have strong core competencies; but unless you're able to work in a team and harness each other's core competen-**

cies, you'll always perform below par because there will always be situations at which you'll do poorly and someone else does well.

Teamwork is mainly about situational leadership, letting the person with the relevant core competency for a situation take leadership.

There are more lessons to be learnt from this story.

Note that neither the hare nor the tortoise gave up after failures. The hare decided to work harder and put in more effort after his failure.

The tortoise changed his strategy because he was already working as hard as he could. In life, when faced with failure, sometimes it is appropriate to work harder and put in more effort. Sometimes it is appropriate to change strategy and try something different. And sometimes it is appropriate to do both.

The hare and the tortoise also learnt another vital lesson. When we stop competing against a rival and instead start competing against the situation, we perform far better.

To sum up, the story of the hare and tortoise teaches us many things. Chief among them are that fast and consistent will always beat slow and steady; work to your competencies; pooling resources and working as a team will always beat individual performers; never give up when faced with failure; and finally, compete against the situation, not against a rival.

Traits of the "New Desirables"

According to the "Future of Work" survey conducted in 2003 by DrakeBeam Morin-Canada Inc. for the *Globe and Mail*, the most employable people in the future will have at least one university degree and a desire to continually acquire more education. A strong understanding of "big picture" issues that affect business and also a base of technical skills that spans specialties will be essential.

The survey says, and here's the rub, leadership potential will outrank technical and personal skills among traits organizations consider most important in an employee. That means employers will expect more capability to work within a team based workplace, better communication skills and more ability to think strategically than they do today.

I know that your instincts already told you what it cost DrakeBeam Morin-Canada Inc. thousands of dollars to find out: Leadership, communication and strategic-thinking are the three traits of the "New Desirables." I hope that *On Fire!* has helped you enhance your quotient of all three.

LIVE IN THE
SWEET
SPOT.

Do Something.

We've come to the end. I hope it's the beginning of a Whole New Level of consistent high performance for you. I want you to achieve a high ROTI – Return On Time Invested – in reading *On Fire!*

So what's the best way to internalize the lessons contained in the preceding pages? What's the best way to turn knowledge into results? How can you begin mastering The Art of Personal Consistency?

You know the answer: do something. Anything. But take action. Do one thing in the next twenty-four hours that propels you forward. In fact, right now, decide on the one thing that you're going to do. Don't close the book until you've decided. Commit to doing it. I mean *really* commit to doing it. Then do it.

Self-Actualization and fulfillment begins with one action. Then another and another. As you know by now, it never gets easier. Becoming Your Personal Best is not an activity you will ever do by rote. But you will keep getting better. And the better you become, the more traction you'll get with each action. And the more traction you get, the more actions you'll take.

It's easier to get motivated than it is to stay motivated. In the few hours you've spent with me, I've played the role of your Coach, Guide, Thought-Sparker, and Entertainer. Now you need to consciously play those roles, both in your life and the lives of others.

Motivation is like food – you need to consume it at least three times a day. And you need to feed it to the people around you if everyone is to remain well nurtured and well nourished. So **just as you would rarely ever starve your body, don't starve your psyche. That's the most important thought I want you to take away with you: fuel your mental hunger for more inspiration and insight. Unlike your stomach, your brain has a limitless appetite.**

When your body needs food, hunger forces you to eat. It's a primal need that must be met. Well, there must be a reason why you've hung in there with me to the very end. Maybe it's the higher part of you that will no longer be denied. Maybe it's a dormant part of you that's been awakened. Maybe it's just time you stepped up to a higher place. Maybe it's nothing more than curiosity about how much of you you have to offer others.

Whatever it is, it's a good thing. Inertia and status quo are never your friends. Complacency is like mental cholesterol. First, it blocks the flow of vitality to your soul. Then it kills you. So stay in flow. Be inquisitive. Act like a person who is always thinking about their Personal Best. And think like a person who is always acting at their Personal Best.

Talk To Me

I know you know something I want to know. I know you have ideas about how to achieve Personal Consistency. I know you're the kind of person I want to connect with. So, in the spirit of making World-Class Friends, contact me:

mike.lipkin@environics.ca
www.mikelipkin.com
416-969-2811
416-969-2822

Ciao for now. I look forward to dialoguing with you when you're ready. Until then, here's my favourite Irish Blessing to send you on your way:

May the road always rise to greet you,
May the wind always be at your back,
May the sun shine gently on your face,
May the rain fall lightly on your fields,
And, until we meet again, may God hold you softly in the palm of his hands,
And may you get to Heaven half an hour before the Devil knows you're dead.

LIVE IN THE
SWEET
SPOT.